NO STONE UNTURNED

*The Life and Times
of Maggie Kuhn*

NO STONE UNTURNED

The Life and Times
of Maggie Kuhn

MAGGIE KUHN

with Christina Long and Laura Quinn

BALLANTINE BOOKS NEW YORK

Library of Congress Cataloging-in-Publication Data
Kuhn, Maggie.
    No stone unturned : the life and times of Maggie Kuhn / Maggie
Kuhn, with Christina Long and Laura Quinn. — 1st ed.
        p.   cm.
    ISBN 0-345-37373-1
    1. Kuhn, Maggie.   2. Social reformers—United States—
Biography.   3. Aged—United States—Political activity.   4. Gray
Panthers.   I. Long, Christina.   II. Quinn, Laura.   III. Title.
HV28.K77A3   1991
361.92—dc20
[B]   91-91859
                                                                          CIP

Text design by Holly Johnson

Manufactured in the United States of America

First Edition: October 1991
10 9 8 7 6 5 4 3 2 1

Contents

Chapter 1	A Thread of Continuity	3
Chapter 2	A Woman's Education	25
Chapter 3	Benevolent Ladies	54
Chapter 4	The Homefront	71
Chapter 5	Hunting Buffalo	92
Chapter 6	A Graceful Exit	118
Chapter 7	Slingshots	143
Chapter 8	Friends and Foes	167
Chapter 9	Shared Housing	193
Chapter 10	Reflections	210
	Bibliography	233

Acknowledgments

My profound appreciation to all the friends, family, colleagues, and collaborators for change who helped make this book possible.

—*Maggie Kuhn*

NO STONE UNTURNED

The Life and Times
of Maggie Kuhn

CHAPTER 1

A Thread of Continuity

As I was standing on a platform at Thirtieth Street Station in Philadelphia the other day, waiting for the Garden State Special to roll down the tracks, I was struck by a vivid image from my childhood. I saw myself, at age four, standing on a train platform with my mother as an enormous steam engine approached, snorting and bellowing huge clouds of smoke. The noise was deafening. I was sure the train would crush us. Overcome with a paralyzing mixture of elation and fear, I stood rooted to the spot until my mother tugged my hand and we climbed onto the train.

As I waited in the Philadelphia station, a ninety-five-pound, eighty-five-year-old woman on her way to Washington, D.C., for a meeting, I felt a semblance of that old excitement. I have always loved a journey and, even now, my bags are almost always packed. There are hazards, of course: escalators make me dizzy, people with large canvas bags over their shoulders nearly knock me to the ground, and the space between the platform and the train seems like a gaping chasm. But the world beckons and I answer.

Over the years, I believe I have climbed aboard almost every type of vehicle this amazing, revolutionary, confounding century has had to offer. As a child, there was nothing more pleasurable to me than riding in the berth of a Pullman car with all its homey touches. Later, I came to appreciate planes just as much. During the 1950s, as a working woman, I frequently traveled in two-seater Piper Cubs, with a pillow and a briefcase wedged between myself and the plane door to keep out the draft.

Once, many years ago, I was flying from Anchorage to Valdez, Alaska, in a six-seater plane. We were flying close to the ground when I happened to look out my window and, to my amazement, saw a big eagle flying alongside us. An eagle! He looked directly at me with his unforgettable, piercing eyes, and his expression seemed to say, "Who is that other bird?"

When I think of that eagle, those old steam engines, and those tiny planes, I marvel at the sweeping changes that have occurred in my lifetime. Of course, my life story and the changes of this century are intertwined. As C. Wright Mills wrote, history and biography intersect; every personal experience is part of a larger story. The advent of the automobile, the women's vote, the Great Depression, World War II, advances in health care, and the prolonging of human life—the procession of history has intimately affected me.

It is not always easy for me to look back on all those years. Contrary to the myth about very old people, I do not spend much time in nostalgic reverie or life review. Like many of my peers, I was taught early on that there are more important things to do than dwell on one's own life. In my parents' household, self-absorption was frowned upon, and we were encouraged to direct our attention to things beyond ourselves, especially in times of adversity.

It is the connection between the personal and the historical that makes telling my story so compelling. I like to think that my private struggles and thoughts provide a window onto a certain era. And because I have been an activist for more than sixty years, perhaps my story will remind people of the important social issues of our century and demonstrate the power of grass-roots efforts.

It has been a century to celebrate. The women's movement, the civil rights movement, and the labor movement have proved that ordinary people can organize and shape the world. For me, a woman born to the task of organizing, it has been a great time to be alive.

I see a deep connection among the past, the present, and the future. I love the inscription set on the cornerstone of the National Archives Building in Washington: "Past Is Prologue." Indeed, in an era of rapid change, we all need to seek meaning in the past, to find its message for the future.

On the wall in my bedroom, there is a photo, taken before I was born, of my Aunt Paulina. There is a certain look in her eye, unfaded even in such an old picture, that reminds me of myself. Indeed, as I look around the room, it seems my past is everywhere. Would Charlotte and Emily Brontë, my two cats, be here if my father had not loved cats? Don't the curtains and the wallpaper show my mother's taste for cheerful order? Would I be in this house at all if it weren't for my grandmother, Margaret Bauer Kooman?

When I am asked to tell a little of my life story, I often start with my grandmother. Though I knew her for only the first five years of my life, I consider her a major influence. She gave me my first sense of what it was to be part of a happy home. My mother's mother was an industrious widow who reigned over a bustling house at 330 Eagle Street in Buffalo. It was a large, roomy house—very much like my home today—with a shiny mahogany banister, a summer and a winter kitchen, an elegant parlor, and a gazebo in the backyard. Two teenage girls, brought over from Germany as hired help, were always dusting and scrubbing, removing the fine layer of soot the coal burner in the basement left on the floor and furniture.

I felt such contentment in that house. In my own home, with just my parents and brother, I was always watched and guarded. But at my grandmother's, the rules were relaxed. I was free to run out to the backyard, explore the attic, hide in the basement. There were often big family dinners, and I loved being one of the crowd. Every sort of family event took place in that house: christenings, holiday celebrations, weddings and funerals. It was not unusual for my father's family to join the activities on Eagle Street. I recall eighteen and twenty children lined up for supper in the dining room: all boys but for my cousin Ruth and me. The chief occupation of the day among the children was riding the banister, and we would all fight and pummel each other to get to the top of the stairs first.

There was a feeling of intimacy among that strange

and wonderful clan. My grandmother, a plump figure dressed in widow's black, sat at the head of the table. Men were treated with great deference, but the house was ruled by women. Before my great-grandmother died, there were four generations of women living there, including my grandmother's younger sister, Aunt Lou; my mother's sister, Aunt Paulina; and Paulina's daughter, Charlotte. They were all widows, except for Charlotte, and they brought order and graciousness to their domestic domain.

There was an independent streak among the women in my grandmother's house. For instance, my Aunt Lou, who was widowed fairly young, was known to have a lover across the Canadian border. Every once in a while, she would go off on a little vacation by herself. It was never openly discussed, but everyone knew where she was going.

I know little of my grandmother's early life except that her parents had emigrated to Buffalo from Amsterdam. As a young woman, she met my grandfather, Leonard Kooman, a merchant from Clymer, a small Dutch community in central New York where the inhabitants replicated the manners and customs of the old country. They were married and, as the story goes, my grandmother brought a trunkful of fancy silk dresses with her to Clymer, never to wear a single one thereafter. Life in Clymer was simple and a sturdy cotton apron was good enough.

My grandfather ran a dry-goods store, and my grandmother, who learned to speak Dutch, made the shirts that were sold in it. Every Sunday my grandfather went to services at Clymer's Dutch Reformed Church. Mealtimes he would bring out his Dutch Bible and pray from it for precisely twenty minutes. When he began to pray, my grandmother would put the potatoes on the stove; when he had finished praying, she knew they were done. Years later, to make me and my cousins laugh, my mother would imitate the booming voice and twitching eyes of her father praying.

My maternal grandparents had two girls and two boys. Walter died in infancy, and John died of appendicitis as a teenager, leaving my mother, Minnie, and her sister, Paulina. In the 1870s my grandparents moved with their two daughters to Buffalo to open a larger store on Seneca Street in the city's Dutch community. The store prospered, but my grandfather's health began to fail. The family bought a gentleman's farm ten miles outside Buffalo in the hope that the country air would help his ailing heart. However, he died a few years later.

After his death everyone expected my grandmother to sell the store, but she was determined to keep it open with help from Paulina and Minnie. In the winter months, when travel was hazardous, my mother and her sister would work in the store during the day and then sleep in the back room at night. In an unusual move for a woman back then, my mother attended the Bryant and Stratton Business College in Buffalo to learn accounting to help in the management of the store. In those days it was extremely rare, if not improper, for women to run a business of their own, and I take some pride in my grandmother's decision to keep the store.

My mother was a bright, capable young woman with dimples and crystal blue eyes. She was famous in the family for her sense of humor. In 1893 she met a young man at the Second Presbyterian Church on Humboldt Parkway. His name was Samuel Kuhn. He was tall and handsome, his eyes so dark they were almost black and his high-button shoes polished to a fashionable gleam. I can picture my parents smiling at each other across the church aisle, their flirtation interfering with their usual concentration on the sermon. They continued their courtship on Delaware Lake, where they skated hand in hand.

My father was twenty-four years old at the time, a hardworking assistant manager in a local credit agency. He was of humble origins. His grandfather had been the mayor of a small town in southern Germany, but lost everything when he fled in the 1840s. Fearing the oppressive rule of the Prussians, my great grandfather left his homeland in the middle of the night, joining the wave of immigrants to this country. He brought his family to East Aurora, New York, outside Buffalo, where my father was later born.

My paternal grandfather, Frederick Kuhn, was a carpenter who struggled to support his wife and ten children in East Aurora. Family legend has it that my grandfather cut off his own leg with a saw after he maimed it badly in a fall from a ladder. I remember sitting on his one leg while posing for a family portrait; the expression on his stern face, buried beneath a white cloud of hair, suggested that the story was true.

My father was the eldest child and, though he rarely discussed it, I imagine that his early life was bleak. Four of his siblings died from diphtheria or scarlet fever as young children. The enmities between German factions followed the family to America. When he was a boy, my father and the other children of southern German families would, for fear of being beaten up, avoid walking through neighborhoods where the northern Germans lived.

As the oldest son, my father was forced to leave high school to go to work to help support the family. He found a job as an office boy and file clerk in Buffalo at the Bradstreet Company, the business and credit reference firm that later merged with its competitor to become Dun and Bradstreet. Extremely intelligent and a quick learner, my father had risen to the post of assistant manager of the Buffalo office by the time he met my mother.

In 1894 my parents married in the parlor at Grand-mother's house. My mother was twenty-seven and my father twenty-four. With her daughters both married, my grandmother sold the dry-goods store and the farm and settled into 330 Eagle Street.

As with all married couples in those days, my parents expected to have their first child right away. When they didn't, their hopes turned into longing. My father was immersed in his work, so I imagine my mother felt the lack of children more than he. But she was a gregarious woman, never prone to brooding or dark thoughts, and she threw herself into church activities and the usual commotion at her mother's house.

By 1903, after ten years of marriage, they were still childless, and as there was little knowledge of infertility then, my mother's doctor gave her no explanation or reason to hope for a pregnancy. However, their lives took a dramatic turn that year when my father was transferred. He was needed to manage the Bradstreet office in Memphis, where the city's cotton farmers and river merchants were providing ample business for the firm. The couple packed their bags, bade farewell to family and friends, and set out for the growing city on the Mississippi. They could have been headed for a foreign country, so different would their new home be from Buffalo.

My mother never felt at home in Memphis, a rough-hewn city known for its vice and corruption, whiskey and prostitution. It was a relatively small city, with a population of about 100,000, but it had five hundred saloons and a homicide rate that was seven times the national average. Buffalo was refined and sophisticated by comparison. My mother was particularly shocked by the disparities between the city's black cotton pickers and domestic servants, who lived in ramshackle dwellings, and their white employers, many of whom occupied stately homes. The city's blacks had barely emerged from slavery, and the white community had a haughty indifference to their decrepit living conditions.

Carrying on a practice in her mother's home, my mother regularly invited her black cleaning woman, Ellie, to eat lunch with her. While Ellie cleaned, my mother made lunch, and then they sat down and ate together in the dining room. I can just imagine her neighbors' indignant whispers: "In the dining room!" This was a serious transgression of the Memphis social code. When my mother's white neighbors found out, they ceased to speak to her. My mother, who thrived on daily interchanges with neighbors, must have felt very alone.

But another turn of events took her mind off her situation. In 1904, the year after they moved to the South and eleven years after they were married, my mother became pregnant. My parents were surprised and cautiously jubilant. My mother was thirty-nine at the time and attributed her first pregnancy to the change in climate. They immediately wrote to relatives up North to tell them the news.

Early on, my mother decided she would not have her first child in Memphis. She felt that having a child there would be a form of acquiescence to the city's segregated way of life. She made up her mind to travel back home to Buffalo to give birth. This was welcome news to my grandmother, who had been pressuring my mother to return home to have the baby. There was great concern about my mother's health, her pregnancy having come at what was then considered an advanced age. In July 1905 my mother took a train to Buffalo, leaving my father behind to see to his duties at the office.

They say the delivery was long and difficult and that my mother barely survived. Nevertheless, on August 3 I was born in my grandmother's front bedroom.

I was named Margaret Eliza, after my two grandmothers. Word was telegraphed to my father, who took the next train to Buffalo. My parents brought me home to Memphis a few weeks later.

With my parents' narrow escape from childlessness, they doted on me in my early years. I remember how lovingly my mother would comb my thick wavy hair, as if she were handling gold threads. She would first brush them and then take a strand and twist it around her finger and mold it there with a comb. She had a special blue "baby book" and lovingly recorded all the little details of my early years: my first celluloid dolly, my first carriage ride, my first pair of white satin shoes. I was the center of my parents' world until I was three years old, when a rival for their attention entered the scene. I remember vividly the day my brother was born. We were staying at my grandmother's house. Being so young, I had only a vague idea of my mother's pregnancy. One day my mother was sequestered in my grandmother's bedroom, and I heard a cry of pain from behind the closed door. I froze. Barely able to breathe, I listened and heard another cry from the bedroom. I panicked. "She's dying!" I thought. I ran down the stairs, through the center hall, out the door, through the front yard, and onto the street. I ran several blocks until I reached Bennett Park, where I curled up on a bench and cried.

I will never forget how bereft I felt there on that hard bench. In a short time my absence was noticed and my Aunt Lou came to take me back to the house and up to my mother's bedside. I practically collapsed again when I saw her alive. I was so relieved that I barely noticed my new brother.

My brother was christened Samuel, after my father. The first year of my brother's life was not tranquil. He was a difficult baby, irritable and sickly. When he was six months old, he came down with pneumonia and almost died. To compound his troubles, a steam kettle that had been set next to him to aid his breathing overturned and burned his neck and face, leaving lifelong scars. I can still remember his incessant cries sounding through the night and the constant strain and anxiety on my parents' faces.

When we returned to Memphis after his birth, I wasn't happy to have someone else occupying my parents' time, and I would often give a sharp kick to the baby carriage. It was during my brother's infancy that my relationship with my father was cemented. While my mother was busy with Sam, my father was in charge of putting me to bed. He would climb under the covers with me and tell me stories about a family of make-believe animals, the Hoo-Hoo cats. They were naughty cats, always getting into trouble, my father animating their exploits with perfect cat cries.

My parents were extremely protective. My mother adhered rigidly to specific hours for our meals and naps and always closely supervised our play. She forbade us to ride bicycles and wagons for fear we would hurt ourselves. We were expected to say our prayers, keep our clothes immaculate, and be mannerly and well behaved.

The task of dressing a child back then was elaborate and time-consuming, and my mother undertook it with painstaking care. I wore long underwear, followed by a pair of stockings that were carefully smoothed over my leggings. A starched cotton and lace dress and black high-button shoes, fastened with a button hook, went on last. Fortunately, I always preferred spending most of my time indoors, reading books and playing with the cats.

We lived in Memphis until I was five, when my father was transferred again, this time to Louisville. My father usually got very short notice for his moves. There would be a crisis at one of the branches and he would be sent to bail it out. He had a reputation for turning around failing offices.

My father would call my mother and say, "The executive called me. I've got to leave by next week." And she would say, "That's fine."

"Well, I'm going ahead to get things straightened out," he would say. And he did, leaving my mother to pack things up and follow with the children.

We traveled often when I was a child. My father was transferred three times and we went to Buffalo for holidays, summer vacations, and between moves. Thus, I spent a great deal of time on trains, which I loved passionately. The trip from Memphis to Buffalo took three days and two nights with a change of trains in Cincinnati.

There is no form of transportation today that compares with riding in a Pullman. In the top compartment over the seat were all the blankets and sheets for two berths, ready for the porter who came to make the beds up at dusk. Miniature hammocks made to fit across the windows held our clothes, and curtains would be buttoned down the windows to shut out the light. I preferred to keep the curtains open.

Some of my happiest moments as a child were spent sitting in a lower berth watching the sights speed by—farmland, rivers, lakes, and towns. I remember seeing fishermen sitting on the ice in upstate New York as I sped by in the overheated cabin of a train; I remember seeing the outline of New York City for the first time. Everything looked smaller from my seat and the feeling was exhilarating. I was no longer Margaret Kuhn, the well-mannered child in a starched frock, but an anonymous spectator, engrossed in each new scene that rushed by. I would often wander down the aisle by myself, stopping to sit for a chat with someone. I was perfectly comfortable with strangers; being on a train together seemed like a bond.

Every year when the weather turned hot in Louisville and we were falling asleep fanning ourselves, my mother, brother, and I took the train to Buffalo, where we spent the summer. A relative would come in a buggy to meet us at the Delaware and Lackawanna Station in Buffalo. In those years Buffalo was a thriving, confident city. I can still see the mules pulling great barges along the Erie Canal and the ships coming into port at the waterfront that stretched for miles, lined with storage elevators that held grain waiting to be transported to other points on the Great Lakes.

I remember the horse-drawn trollies that carried people across town and went up and down my grand-

mother's street. Teams of stocky horses pulled cars
that looked like small vans with seats along the sides.
In the wintertime the floor was covered with straw to
keep passengers' feet from freezing; the horses wore
heavy wool blankets, buckled around the middle. In
the summer the horses wore straw bonnets lined with
damp sponges to protect their heads from the blazing
sun. Their long ears poked up through holes in the
bonnets and gave them a coquettish look as they
shook their heads to keep the flies away.

It was during my long summers in Buffalo that I got
to know some of the people in my extended family.
One person, in particular, had a profound effect on
me: Aunt Paulina, or "Aunt Pline," as we called her.
A small, dark-haired woman with intense blue eyes,
Aunt Pline was a Sunday school teacher who taught
me how to read, using Bible stories as my primers. She
was extremely religious and hardworking, and yet always seemed in high spirits. Even when she was an old
woman, she would run along the beach, kicking up her
skirts and laughing hilariously.

I always thought her gaiety was a sign of great inner
fiber, considering the hardship and tragedy in her life.
When Aunt Pline was a young woman, she fell in love
with John Lennon, an engineer on one of the passen-
ger trains of the Old New York Central Railroad that
went from New York City to Buffalo to Chicago. The
match was vehemently opposed by her father, apparently because my grandfather looked down on a simple railroad worker. The couple exchanged passionate
love letters in which they vowed to remain faithful to

one another. I suppose they were waiting for my grandfather's death.

When he died a short time later, the couple made plans to marry. They had to wait for three years, however, the proper mourning period among Dutch Calvinists. Three years to the day after my grandfather's death, they married, moving to a boarding home to start their new life.

After all that waiting, their time together was brief. Two years after they were married and a few months after Pline gave birth to a daughter, there was a terrible wreck in the Buffalo rail yard. His train plunged through a closed switch, trapping Uncle John between two cars. He was severely burned and died a few hours later. The one and only love of Pline's life was gone.

Aunt Pline and her daughter, Charlotte, were left penniless. My aunt sought compensation from the railroad company, but it refused to give a single cent, even for funeral expenses, to injured crew members. The railroad brotherhoods were just beginning to form in those days and workers were still relatively unprotected. Eventually the matter went to the courts, where it was ruled that the switchman was at fault in the accident. Under the Fellow Servant Act, the company could not be held liable for accidents caused by its employees.

This experience changed Paulina forever. In those days the plight of a young widow was often desperate. Paulina was forced to move back to my grandmother's house, never again to have a home of her own. Though she never spoke bitterly of her situation, she was

politicized, becoming keenly aware of the powerlessness of women and children. During the next twenty
years, Paulina was a regular at rallies and meetings of
Buffalo's suffragettes. At one of these rallies, my aunt
made the bold move of taking off her hat, a public act
considered unseemly in those days, as a show of rebellion. I credit her—and the legions of other women
who shared her sense of quiet outrage—with changing
the world. Women's voting rights were hotly debated
in Buffalo for many years until finally, in 1917, New
York State granted women the vote. Three years later
a constitutional amendment legitimized the women's
vote nationwide.

In the years that I visited Buffalo as a child, I knew
little of Pline's political work. She was my friend. My
grandmother owned several properties in Buffalo that
she rented out. After she died, Aunt Pline supervised
their upkeep. I loved to accompany her on the first of
the month as she went to collect the rents. Walking
this way and that through the neighborhood, we
would stop and knock at each of the tenants' doors.
My aunt, who was always on friendly terms with the
renters, often would be invited in for a cup of coffee.
I had a great curiosity about how other people lived,
so while she chatted, my eyes drank up every detail.
Was that a picture of a bridge on the wall? To whom
was that letter on the table addressed? Why was that
man's shoe untied? As we left each house, my aunt
would spy a leaky gutter or a broken step, and I could
see her making mental notes about the repairs. I think
I learned from her a respect for detail, a thoroughness

that my friends at college would make fun of when they glanced at my copious lecture notes.

Aunt Pline and Aunt Lou were both models to me in later life, demonstrating to me that a woman could lead a full life without a mate. My mother, on the other hand, deferred to my father. Though he adored her, he believed he was the absolute ruler of the house. He kept strict control over all the money that was spent, so she had to ask each time she needed cash. He was a brooding man, and if he didn't get his way, he was apt to sulk for several days, refusing to speak to anyone. Like many women in her position, my mother was a brilliant diplomat, skillful at getting what she wanted without appearing to demand it. If anyone could persuade my father to change his mind it was she.

My father also respected my mother's judgment, and he eagerly sought her advice about hiring. When he interviewed a job candidate, he would arrange for my mother to show up at the office on some false pretext, staying for the few minutes she needed to size up the prospect. My parents would talk it over that night and my father always went with her choice.

My father was the consummate company man. Corporate America blossomed on the backs of men like him, with their willingness to leave their families and travel at a moment's notice, their penchant for blaming themselves rather than the company when things went wrong, their belief that the company's success would make the world a better place. He loved having me visit him at work. I remember how he beamed when he showed me the new copying device he had introduced at one of his offices.

My father believed everyone could achieve success no matter how deprived his beginnings. He disapproved of his brother Frank, because he was always involved in fly-by-night businesses. At one point Frank owned a small brewery, Kuhn's Beer, which opened outside Buffalo just as Prohibition ended. My father didn't like the family name attached to a common brewery and he was annoyed by his brother's never-ending financial hardship. He refused Frank loans. My father got along much better with his brother Joe, who owned a successful printing company.

Because he didn't have one himself, my father valued a proper education above all else in life. Despite his lack of formal schooling, he was one of the most learned men I have ever known. In his spare time he taught himself Latin, Greek, and higher mathematics. He had a passion for abstruse theological debate and was a student of Presbyterian law and doctrine.

We moved to an apartment in Louisville. Shortly thereafter, I started school. I was a good child who always tried to please my parents. As I grew older, I began to notice that my mother was much older than the mothers of other children. I often thought of that afternoon at my grandmother's house and her wail of pain. I would lie awake at night, wondering what would happen to me if she were to die. In those moments I resolved to do everything I could to make her happy.

Early on I endeared myself to my father by being a quick learner. I loved to read. I think my father saw in me the child he might have been if he hadn't grown up as one of ten children in a poor home. While I was a joy to him, Sam was a burden. Sam continued to be a sickly child, suffering from constant respiratory problems. Several times a high fever sent him into convulsions, filling us with fear.

My father, who had seen so many of his own siblings die, was distressed by his son's frailty. Unlike at work, where his diligence and drive made a difference, at home there was nothing he could do to help Sam. His sense of powerlessness made him impatient.

Sam's problems were not just physical. He was very timid and fearful, always clutching my mother whenever we left the house. When he turned five, he became extremely apprehensive about the prospect of attending kindergarten. "Couldn't I stay at home?" he would whimper. "All children go to school," my father would reply, believing that the best way to combat Sam's fears was to dismiss them and belittle him.

On Sam's first day of kindergarten, my mother walked the two of us to school. I was starting the third grade that day and was eager to get to class. Fearful of being separated from Mother, Sam held her arm tightly the whole way. He began to cry when we arrived. I kissed him good-bye and headed for my class.

A short time later, as I sat before my new teacher, I was startled to see Sam appear at the door of the classroom. He was soaking wet. His pants, his stockings, his shoes—everything was dripping. The teacher excused me and I took his hand and walked him to the girls' room. Apparently, my brother had fallen into a urinal. I was mortified and, worse than that, ashamed of my embarrassment. I dried him off as best I could and then waited with him until my mother came to take him back home.

My attitude toward him changed permanently that day. I no longer saw him as a rival for my parents' affections. He was now "my little brother" and I became as fiercely protective of him as my mother was. While I excelled in school, Sam did not adjust well to his new environment. He was a bright child but ill at ease with strangers. He was always tearful and anxious when my mother left him at the school door at the start of the day.

Every night I would help him with his homework and every day I would walk him to school. During the course of the day, I would think up excuses to walk by his classroom and peer in to see how he was doing. He often appeared lost and unhappy. When Sam received a bad report card, I would plead with my father not to scold him. "I will help him do better," I would say. After my schoolwork was done, I would sit down and help Sam with his assignments.

We stayed in Louisville for five years, then the company called on my father to relocate to Cleveland to manage the Bradstreet office there. As usual, it was my mother's responsibility to pack the trunks. I remember her immersed in the task: washing, ironing, and folding the clothes, wrapping toys and other valuables so they wouldn't break. Two days before our departure, a delivery man would knock at the door and heave our trunks into the hold of his truck. My brother and I would pack a small bag of supplies to carry us through: some clothes and a few books.

When we arrived at our destination, we would identify the trunks at the train station, and another man would deliver them to the house or a hotel a day or two later. I always felt a mixture of apprehension and anticipation as the trunks were opened. Once I found my favorite doll smashed, its hand-painted china head cracked right down the middle. More often I was relieved to find so much of my familiar life transported intact.

CHAPTER 2

A Woman's Education

If I were a lady and all of that,
I shouldn't go on Euclid without a hat.
CLASS SONG, 1926, COLLEGE FOR WOMEN,
WESTERN RESERVE UNIVERSITY

My mother was always sympathetic to the predicament of a fidgety child in an uncomfortable church
pew. Each Sunday, at the beginning of the sermon, she
would hand me a small box of pins and a pincushion.
While my parents turned their attention to the pulpit,
I became engrossed in a tiny world of my own. I
transferred the pins, one by one, from the box to the
cushion. Then I made little designs—flowers, birds,
butterflies—with the brightly colored heads of the
pins. After a while I transferred them back to the box,
again slowly, as if I were performing a surgical procedure. It was an exacting ritual from which I would
never deviate. In its own way it was like a prayer.

Above all else, mine was a churchgoing family. I
cannot remember missing a Sunday for any reason
other than dire illness. When my family moved to a
new city, the search for the right church was more
important than the search for the perfect house or
school.

Attending church was not just a spiritual duty. It
was a social rite and an opportunity to participate in

public affairs. Presbyterianism, with its elaborate form of government, appealed to my father's sense of order and justice. Wherever we went to church, he was extremely active, diligently working his way up in the ranks of the laity. I can still remember the expression on his face on those Sundays when he served communion—a privilege reserved for the elders who served on the "session," the church's governing body. He truly glowed with pride and piety.

My father preferred large Presbyterian churches that attracted distinguished pastors and leaders of the business community. When I look back on my family's years in Cleveland, where I lived from the ages of twelve to twenty-four, I immediately envision the gray sandstone tower of the Old Stone Church, a bastion of wealth and antiquity in the heart of Cleveland. I can still hear the church's chimes ringing out across Public Square and see the pews filled with women in fancy hats and fur coats, and straight-backed men who exuded confidence, ability, sometimes arrogance. I can see its barrel-vaulted ceiling and the Tiffany stained-glass windows, and I can hear the majestic sound of its organ, which sounded to my young ears like the most remarkable instrument in the world. Old Stone's organ was so loved by the church members that recitals were offered during the week to give businessmen a reason to come to the church at lunchtime. I would stand with the congregation during the closing hymn, feeling a surge of reverence and awe.

We sat in Pew 72, surrounded by Cleveland's elite. I remember Ambrose Swasey, his thick white eyebrows visible as he bent over his prayer book. The partner of Warner and Swasey Co., which manufactured machine tools and astronomical instruments, he was president of the Cleveland Chamber of Commerce, director of two Cleveland banks, and trustee of Western Reserve University.

William Hopkins, the councilman and later city manager of Cleveland whom my father came to respect deeply, attended the church. A former bookkeeper who grew up in Newburgh, Cleveland's gritty iron ward, Hopkins was just the kind of self-made man my father gravitated toward. Ed Williams, president of Sherman Williams, the paint manufacturer, was also a member. With men like these on its rolls, the church influenced the cultural, business, and civic life of the city.

The man who drew many of these influential people together at a time when Cleveland's more prominent citizens were moving to the suburbs was Andrew B. Meldrum, a big-hearted, blustery man who served as pastor of Old Stone for twenty-five years. Meldrum frequently ventured into Cleveland's rougher neighborhoods to speak before community organizations. His sermons were so popular they were reprinted in little booklets for distribution throughout the city.

My father expected to be moved and stimulated by a sermon and only the most literate and incisive preachers moved him. My father said Meldrum made "his hearers feel that he was voicing the deepest desires of their hearts." The two men shared a philos-

ophy that glorified the individual and his ability to rise
above his circumstances.

Meldrum called it "clear grit." In one of his sermons in 1915, he explained:

> Grit is not a pretty word, to be sure, but it
> denotes a splendid characteristic. It represents
> that "percentage of iron in a man's tempera-
> ment that gives stability and permanence to his
> character." It is what someone has called "the
> steel rod in his backbone" that prevents him
> from bending to every prompting or impulse
> or gust of opinion. When a man has this vir-
> tue, no matter what his failings may be, you
> may entrust a duty to him confident that he
> will see it through.

The same "steel rod" was my father's virtue, but his
intolerance of those who did not possess it made him
a difficult, uncompromising man.

Meldrum didn't glorify the material successes of
his followers. "What we call success is only the
shuck," he said. "Life's value is what develops inside.
The greatest thing about a man is his soul." But he did
glorify those qualities of strength and perseverance
that had made many of the men of Old Stone brilliant
successes in life.

I remember having Sunday lunch at the home of
Elliot Whitlock, a member of Old Stone and a civil
engineer who had been hired by Hopkins to conduct
a three-year study of the city's growing pollution

problem. Back then, industry flourished in Cleveland with the manufacturing of hardware, paints, electrical apparatus, bridges, printing presses, car wheels, chemicals, sewing machines, bolts and nuts, washers, and rivets. But the great factories along the Cuyahoga River, which ran into Lake Erie, used the river as a dumping ground for their refuse and steel mills belched thick, choking soot into the air. I'll never forget how everything—park benches, porches, cars—was covered with black grime.

We would all go over to the Whitlocks' house and sit on their front porch, which overlooked Lake Erie, and wonder and worry about its future. The river was already heavily polluted and you could smell its noxious vapors across town. Mr. Whitlock would explain to us the methods and equipment that could be used to reduce pollutants in the air and water. It was Whitlock and Hopkins who recommended that the city's industrial giants take steps to curtail the pollution. Cleveland's leading businessmen refused to cooperate.

Since the problems of the city became the concerns of the church, discussion about the pollution spilled over into meetings of the church session. As much as my father admired Old Stone's businessmen, he spoke out in defense of Hopkins' plan. He argued for their compliance on theological grounds, saying that "as stewards of the creation" they were under God's judgment to protect the earth. Ed Williams defended his company's dumping of lead resins into the river, arguing that it would cleanse itself through the action of the currents and the sun shining on it. The sun shining! Even then that sounded preposterous. Furthermore, he said, his customers would not pay the costs of alternative disposal. My father, who had become clerk of session and treasurer of the church, got into many angry discussions with Williams.

Williams and his wife sat in the pew adjoining ours, which made it impossible to avoid them in church. When we saw them, they would bow in a civil manner and so would we, but no words were exchanged. Afterward the two families would always keep their distance.

It was inconceivable to us then that the plan for pollution control would not be approved, but the city lacked the courage to face down men like Williams. Forty years later, Lake Erie was a mass of industrial waste, most of its fish had died, and the beaches were littered with refuse and closed to the public.

Like Buffalo, Cleveland was a prospering industrial city in those early decades of the twentieth century. Bustling stores lined Euclid Avenue; suburbs were springing up on either side of the Cuyahoga River—Cleveland's lifeline. From 1909 to 1919, the city's population grew by 42 percent to a total of 796,800. An enormous working class had sprung up, with twenty-nine nationalities represented among the newcomers who came for jobs. The Cleveland International Airport, the Cleveland Public Library, the magnificent Public Auditorium, and office buildings such as the seventeen-story Union National Bank were all erected while we lived in Cleveland. I remember the movie houses that sprung up along Euclid Avenue: the Stillman, the Allen, the State, and the Ohio.

We lived in a spacious Colonial brick house on Lake Avenue on the West Side of Cleveland overlooking Edgewater Park and Lake Erie. It was the first place, outside Buffalo, that seemed like a real home to us. During the summer we would walk across Edgewater Park to swim at Perkins Beach, a pebble beach. I swam in sneakers to keep from cutting my feet on the stones; and I watched big long freighters carrying iron and coal on Lake Erie from the deck of the cruise liner we took up the Great Lakes every summer. I was in awe of that chain of inland seas.

My family bought our first car in Cleveland, a big blue Westcott. My mother did all the driving. My father didn't like to drive; he was not mechanically inclined. He could garden but he could not repair anything. He was an excellent manager, but he never fixed a faucet.

My mother had driven a horse and carriage in Buffalo and she had no problem making the transition to a car. She was a fairly small woman, and I remember how impressed I was seeing her climb into the driver's seat. She knew exactly what to do. The only time I remember any difficulty was when we later moved to Philadelphia and she was required to parallel park. She was not comfortable driving backward.

In the winter Sam loved to play in Edgewater Park. He was always happiest in the cold weather, when he was on a pond with his ice skates or coasting down a hill on his sled.

The contrast between Sam and me was becoming

even more apparent. While Sam was barely passing at school, I was at the top of my class and its youngest member, having skipped a grade in elementary school. I was clearly my father's favorite and as I entered my teenage years this made me feel more and more uneasy. Whenever Sam came home with a bad report card, I would defend him and argue that my parents should support him, not chastise him. But my father blamed Sam. He always believed Sam was not trying hard enough. "If he had the will to do better, he could," my father would say. My mother was on Sam's side and would tell my father, "You don't understand him. He's just a little boy. Give him a chance."

For a long time, I could do no wrong in my father's eyes. Our relationship grew more strained, however, when I became interested in boys. I was fairly shy in high school, but I did stir some interest from the opposite sex. Today, when sex is so much more open than it was when I was a child, the value of a good kiss has been forgotten. Back then when someone kissed you for the first time it was something you never forgot. The first person I kissed was Henry Christian, the son of a Cleveland contractor and a classmate at West High School. To me that first kiss was a turning point. It stirred my first erotic desire. My goodness, those sensations were so intense!

I loved to ride in Henry's Model A Ford, looking up at the sky and the stars and feeling the exhilarating wind blowing through my hair. When we stopped to park, there was a moment of awkwardness when the only sound was the car seat squeaking as we moved closer to each other. The awkwardness dissolved as soon as we embraced and began to thoroughly explore each other's bodies.

The first time Henry came to our home, I was puzzled by my father's behavior. He was rude and cold, refusing to rise to greet the young man. In all other situations, my father was a most mannerly and gracious man, but when a young man knocked at our door, his personality went through visible changes. It wouldn't matter much what the young man was like or what he did for a living. In the years to come, my father would give all my suitors the cold shoulder.

The rules governing my social life were strict. If I wasn't in by ten o'clock, my father would come and get me. At that age there is nothing more humiliating than having your father appear before you at a party and demand that you follow him home.

In 1922, at the age of sixteen, I was graduated from West High School with honors. I wanted to attend a college in the East, preferably Wellesley or Vassar. I was eager for new experience and part of me wanted to flee the growing tension over my brother. But my future was to be a family decision and my parents were not ready to relinquish me. My father was determined that I stay in Cleveland and attend the College for Women at Western Reserve University.

The college, attended by the daughters of Cleveland's affluent families, was located in Cleveland's East side, a pleasant community of tree-lined streets and Victorian homes. It had close ties to Old Stone, where many of the college's benefactors and faculty members preached and worshipped. While many of the other girls at the college were "streetcar" students who returned home to their parents at the end of the day, my mother and father agreed to let me live on campus in a concession to my desire for independence.

In those days higher education for women was still in its adolescence. We were given two career options—nursing and teaching—and it was expected that any career would be interrupted early on for marriage. I majored in English literature with minor studies in sociology and French.

I count myself lucky for not having been born sooner, when perhaps I would have had no higher education at all. The birth of female education at Western Reserve was a tortuous process. Just thirty years earlier, the College for Women was not in existence and Cleveland's young women fought a determined battle to gain admission to Adelbert College, the university's college for men. The records of the dispute seem humorous in retrospect, so extreme were the arguments against educating women.

In the late 1800s Adelbert's president, Carroll Cutler, an enlightened Presbyterian minister, took the bold step of admitting women to the college. During the next nineteen years, forty-three women enrolled—hardly a threat to the male majority—and nineteen graduated. Many faculty members, trustees, and students of the college were uneasy with Cutler's policy. Some young men feared that women would take over, and the girls were fond of teasing them about their fears. As college historian C. H. Cramer recounts, the school's first female sorority claimed—jokingly, of course—that it had asked its initiates to take the following pledge: "I, Nancy Flutterbut, do hereby solemnly promise to do all in my power to keep secret all that transpires within these walls; to put forth my best endeavors to transform this college into a female seminary, and to treat with the utmost contempt all such male students as the devil shall cause to cross my path."

In 1884 the faculty petitioned the trustees to deny women admission. They claimed that the women would drive all the men away and that the college would be wasted on mere women. Cutler staunchly opposed them.

The board of trustees voted in favor of the college president. The day after their action, however, the young men boycotted classes. The women gleefully hung a banner, proclaiming "Adelbert Female Seminary," from the window of the main college building.

The faculty, which also feared for the moral welfare of its male students who would share classes with women, persisted in its fight against coeducation. In 1886 Cutler resigned. His successor, Rev. Hiram Collins Haydn, a minister at Old Stone, was chosen because of his opposition to the presence of women at the school. Less than two months into his term in January 1888, Haydn called the women students to his

home and informed them that coeducation at Adelbert would be terminated, advising them that they
would be better off in a women's college, where their
"special needs, interests, and mentality could be taken
into account."

That same year, in response to the outcry from
proponents of coeducation, the university opened the
College for Women, offering it no financial support. It
opened in September 1888 in a farmhouse at Euclid
Avenue and Adelbert Road. There were fourteen students. The first gymnasium, set up in a barn behind
the dormitory, was equipped with a few dumbbells
and a rowing machine. The gym instructor came when
she could.

In 1891 the college granted a diploma to its first
graduate, a transfer student from Wellesley. Commencement exercises were held in the Calvary Presbyterian Church, where Professor George Herbert
Palmer, a noted educator and philosopher from Harvard, gave a speech appropriately titled "The Glory of
the Imperfect."

The college grew quickly with the help of some of
Cleveland's leading philanthropists, including Louis
H. Severance and Flora Stone Mather, for whom the
college was later named.

By 1922, when I enrolled, it had more than four
hundred students. I can still see my classmates with
their bobbed hair and needlepoint slippers shuffling
across campus, hampered somewhat by the tight fit of
their skirts. I can remember surreptitiously smoking
my first cigarette sitting on one of the squeaky wicker

chairs in Guilford House, the dorm where I shared a suite with Marge Yarian, the school's tennis champion. I can picture the elegant sterling silver tea set with which my classmates and I were served tea in Haydn Hall. And I remember the streetcar conductor who, when the trolley stopped at Euclid Avenue and Bellflower Road, would announce, "Ladies College for Women."

We were governed strictly, more so than the men—a holdover from the period when it was believed that women would bring immorality to university life. We had to wear gloves and hats when off campus at all times. We signed in and out of our dorm. The house matron met our dates at the door and instructed them to wait in the parlor until we came to greet them. The doors were locked promptly at 10:00 P.M. Three late returns would place the student under "house arrest"—no off-campus nights for at least a week.

We also were required to attend chapel four times a week. I remember how we made fun of the ritual in a ditty:

O unknown power, whose eccentric whims
Four times a week select our chapel hymns
For years we've suffered, hear at length our plea
When will you give us some variety?

Four times a week our lagging voices rise,
As we drawl out hymn 755,
Ten years ago, the school wailed loud and long,
For even then, they sang the same old song.

Reserve may change, new powers will hold sway,
Students and faculty will pass away
But years from now, we'll pass the chapel door
And hear the same old hymn forever more.

For our gym course, which was taught by an elderly "Miss May," we would dress in navy blue serge bloomers, stockings, and middy blouses—a uniform not very conducive to free movement.

The college had a profound commitment to academic excellence and provided a rigorous curriculum. There were great scholarly women on the faculty and in the administration who were models for us all. They were constrained, however, by the lingering belief that women should not delve too deeply into abstruse subjects and should be equipped for marriage. We took courses in English literature and chemistry but also studied child care and home economics.

Before college I had not received any sex education. My parents never once discussed reproduction with me. I learned the rudimentary facts from experience with young men and from my biology class. Biology was one of our mandatory courses; we learned the function of the major bodily organs as well as how to care for the bedridden. It started immediately after gym, requiring that I change from gym clothes into street clothes in a matter of minutes. To appear on the street in a gym outfit would, of course, have been tantamount to appearing naked and would have landed a young woman in the dean's office. I remember running to my dorm, changing into street clothes, and then racing to the Adelbert Campus, where Dr.

Bean taught Biology I to both men and women.

Dr. Bean was a shy Bostonian with a deep New England accent, and I suspect this was one of his first teaching assignments. He never looked at the roomful of young women before him and wore a visor to protect himself further from our inquiring eyes. The class was all lecture, and our grades were determined solely by how well we absorbed his lectures. In discussing the circulatory system, he talked at length about the "aorter." When it came up on a test, all of us spelled it the way we had heard it. He was furious! He thought we were making fun of him and flunked us all on the test.

One of my favorite courses was Sociology, given by Professor Gehlke. It was my introduction to the societal and class structure in America and the relationship of institutions to that structure. I was inspired by the early great thinkers in the field: Auguste Comte, Karl Marx, and Max Weber. They were not at all like today's sociologists, who try to reduce human behavior to clinical studies with their statistics and graphs. Those early thinkers believed sociologists should not only explain society but work to change it.

Professor Gehlke took us to Cleveland's jails, social welfare institutions, sweatshops, and slums to expose his sheltered students to some of the city's harsher realities. Some of my classmates took a rather irreverent view of these trips. I remember the song they wrote about them:

> Tramp, tramp, tramp the class is marching,
> through the corridors of jails,

through the wards of hospitals,
hanging desperately on Gehlke's coattails.

Tramp, tramp, tramp the class is marching,
cheer up girls, we're nearly through,
someday they'll be a strike
because of such a hike,
and what will Gehlke do?

We visited Cleveland's growing slums, observing frayed, rat-infested houses with no plumbing and whole neighborhoods I had never known existed. It was just a glimpse into another world—like my visits to Aunt Pline's tenants—but I could not forget those houses. They lit a spark in my conscience that made me eager to know more about the people who lived there.

I couldn't get those images out of my mind. I would return home from the field trips and tell my father that the city's poor were neglected, underpaid, and exploited. For the first time, my father and I strongly disagreed. My father was the quintessential man of his generation and class. He believed everyone could pull themselves up by their bootstraps and the poor were poor because they didn't work hard enough. He was absolutely furious at me and accused me of expounding theories that were "disloyal" and "antisocial."

My father and I were in agreement, however, about what I was learning in my biblical literature class. The course was taught by the Reverend Howell

Merriman Haydn, the son of Hiram Haydn, who had banned women from the college back in 1888. An ordained Presbyterian minister who frequently took the pulpit in the summer months at Old Stone, Professor Haydn was a fervent and dynamic lecturer, who came to class on crutches, having apparently been crippled by polio. My father was thrilled that he was my instructor.

My father was quite liberal theologically and thus strongly agreed with Professor Haydn's arguments against fundamentalism. At that time it was still somewhat novel for a minister to argue that the Bible need not be read literally, that the stories of Adam and Eve, the Tower of Babel, Cain and Abel had value because of their symbolic meaning. When approached in this intellectual way, biblical literature satisfies the mind as well as the spirit. Faith is more than blind devotion, Dr. Haydn taught us. His course—more than any sermons or church services—ensured my commitment to my religion by giving me the freedom to question it.

I was an honors student in college, though not on the same level as my roommate, who was never distracted from her studies. I believe there are three things every college student should accomplish: she should learn to think, she should have fun, and she should fall in love. I did all three.

In my sophomore year I was invited to join the Gamma Delta Tau sorority. The sororities were small at the college, only fifteen or twenty members. Chapters of national sororities were prohibited on campus, as was stipulated by Flora Stone Mather when she endowed the college. Apparently, Mather was rejected from the sorority of her choice when she attended a women's college in the East.

The sororities were not permitted to meet on campus, and so we had our weekly meetings at the home of one of the members. They were convivial evenings with prayer, song, and conversation. At the beginning of the year, we held a sunrise breakfast at the Edgewater Hotel overlooking Lake Erie to initiate new members. At the end of the year, the sorority hosted a formal dance, a chance for everyone to bring out their raccoon coats and formal dresses.

I frequently went home for weekend visits and to attend Old Stone Sunday services. While I was at college, Rev. Meldrum left the pastorate of Old Stone, to the dismay of many Clevelanders. He was succeeded by William Hiram Foulkes.

I do not remember a great deal about Rev. Foulkes himself, but I clearly remember his son. The pastor's family sat two pews in front of us at church, and Paul Foulkes, a tall, dark young man who sported a derby hat, immediately caught my eye. Since my father was the clerk of session, my family frequently came in contact with the pastor's family. Paul and I became friendly.

Paul was three years older than I was and had already graduated from college. He was considered something of a black sheep in his family for he had no definite career plans and was not following his father into the ministry.

Paul and I did not date each other in the conventional sense. We had a passionate romance. During the first semester of my junior year, we went out together almost every night. He soon began to write me a letter every day—long, ardent declarations of love—and bestowed many little gifts upon me. At times I had a sneaking suspicion that I was one of a series of love obsessions, but I was flattered by his attentions and equally infatuated.

The college curfew unfortunately cut short our interludes in Wade Park, where we found secluded spots to make love. I enjoyed sex and I never questioned my right to it. I was not a fearful young woman. When Paul and I began to have sex, I did not fret over the loss of my virginity.

My sorority sisters surmised that Paul and I were having an *adult* romance and it caused them alarm. The year before, a pregnant sorority member had left the college in shame. "You just can't get pregnant, Margaret!" one trembling sorority sister told me. "The honor of the sorority hangs on it!" Others pleaded in the same manner. I took action.

I went to a gynecologist and told him I was on the verge of marriage and was not prepared to have children. I suppose if I had lived in a small town where everyone knew everyone else, this would have been impossible. But I was in a big, bustling city that granted some anonymity. I left the doctor's office with my first diaphragm.

Thus our romance continued unabated. I told my parents nothing of the affair. My father didn't think highly of Paul, and it would have seemed improper, given our fathers' positions, for us to have been involved. I was not ecstatic when Paul asked me to elope, but I agreed. Unless we could carry it off secretly, it would mean the end to my education. College enrollment was forbidden to married women.

We decided to marry at Christmastime. When the school term ended Paul and I went to city hall to obtain a marriage license. According to our plan, we would elope on the day my family had made plans to travel to Buffalo for the holidays. My parents were to board the train at the old depot and I was to board at the station near the college. As the hour for the train's departure approached, I had deep misgivings about the whole marriage scheme. I was not so madly in love as I thought, or perhaps I was simply too pragmatic. I worried about how we would support ourselves. Above all I realized I loved school and wanted an education more than anything. And I was not ready to break with my family. I grabbed my bag and headed for the station to catch the train to Buffalo. I remember climbing aboard, breathless and exhausted, and greeting my parents as if nothing unusual had transpired.

Even though I had not married Paul, our romance marked a turning point in my relations with my family. I had begun to lead a double life. Several weeks later I broke down in tears and told my mother the whole story. It came as no surprise to her. Like many mothers, she had a sixth sense when it came to her children, and all along she had suspected that I was having an affair. She put her arms around me.

"It was so hard not to tell you," I said.

"I know, I know," my mother said soothingly. While she did not approve, she understood me and loved me. She warned me never to tell my father. My mother knew how to appease my father, yet still affirm her children. On that day I knew we were not just mother and daughter, but friends. I have cherished our friendship all my life. Many women and their mothers have an undercurrent of tension, perhaps a rivalry, between them. But with us, there were many occasions when our warm feelings for each other sustained us both.

My romance with Paul had cost me Phi Beta Kappa, but I was still a good student. I returned to school after the Christmas break with renewed interest in my studies. I had decided I would be a teacher. Teaching was one profession open to me as a woman, and so, giving little thought to the matter, I began completing the course work. But when I was exposed to the work of John Dewey, the great philosopher and educator, I began truly to want to be a teacher.

I think I always had a passion for reform; it's in my blood. Dewey's efforts to upset the traditions of the classroom excited me. To Dewey, learning need not be forced. Teachers were most likely to succeed, he believed, if they took advantage of a child's natural curiosity. You learn by doing.

I remembered from my own early school days how much more quickly I learned when teachers made a subject come alive for us. When our fifth grade class did an arithmetic problem in which we had to calculate how to hang wallpaper in a fictitious room, I was completely at sea. I saw no sense in the procedure when one could simply call in a paper hanger and let him do the figuring. It was plain drudgery to work these problems and I loathed them. The rest of the students felt pretty much the same way until one day the teacher had the happy idea to let us paper a dollhouse according to the rules of the problem. Every one of us sat up and took notice and began to like those problems better than any other kind. Work had become play because we understood it, were interested in it, and loved to do it.

I remembered how too many of my teachers had demanded that we learn by memorization or by formulas and rules. A high school English teacher gave us a dozen passages of *Macbeth* to memorize before we had even read the play! In a high school physics laboratory, we were required to make extremely complicated drawings of parts of the steam and gas engines, though the principles of the mechanical action of these machines were too advanced for our class. The beautiful diagrams and wonderfully artistic drawings we made showed little more than the ability to handle a ruler and colored inks successfully.

I was impassioned about Dewey; the world seemed a mere laboratory for his ideas. When I read about American education today, his teachings seem as alive and relevant to me as they did then. In my senior year I began my first practice teaching at Fairmount Junior High School, near campus. After observing experienced teachers for several weeks, one day I was left alone in the classroom. My first assignment was to teach a grammar lesson to ninth graders. What could be more dull? It was the perfect opportunity to put Dewey's theories to the test. I thought it out a bit and then decided to make the day's lesson come alive by dividing the class into teams and turning the lesson into a relay race. The first team would go to the blackboard and underline the subject of a sentence, the second group would underline the verb, another the verb modifiers, and so on.

Suddenly, the classroom was full of activity: the students were overjoyed to be playing a game. I felt the thrill of guiding young minds.

Just when things were progressing, however, an altercation developed between two students. I tried in vain to establish order by stomping my feet and clapping. More students joined in the fight, throwing erasers and notebooks.

What would John Dewey have advised? I picked up an eraser and threw it at the offending students. Just then, my supervising teacher walked into the room. The students froze in their tracks. I grew pale. A sudden chill settled over my career.

After class my superviser gave me a lecture about discipline and order, advising me not to become too friendly with the students. In her book that was not the way to maintain an orderly classroom. "I'm not going to fail you," she told me at the close of the semester. "But I'm not going to give you anything higher than a 'C.'"

The competition for teaching assignments was

such that a "C" was tantamount to failure. The day I
learned of my grade, I took the trolley home, arriving
on my parents' doorstep in tears. I knew my mother
would understand, but my father was surprisingly
sympathetic. "It's not the end of the world," he said.
"Why don't you take some time to reflect and explore
other career options?" I loved him for that. My father
was ambitious for me, which made his sympathy all
the more important.

In 1926, not long after I graduated with honors from
college and reluctantly moved back home, my "Aunt"
Cora, a friend of the family, invited me to visit the
central offices of the Cleveland Young Women's
Christian Association at Prospect Avenue and East
Eighteenth Street. There was a constant bustle about
the Y building—women coming and going at every
hour of the day. Cleveland's lower-class women—the
women who lived in the city neighborhoods that I
visited for my sociology class—came to the Y for en-
tertainment, relaxation, education, Christian values,
an inexpensive meal, and a place to sleep. It was sort
of a second home for them. When you walked
through its hallways, you could hear a dozen conversations, noise from the swimming pool, and various
meetings in session. There was a combination of seriousness and lightheartedness about the place.

It was here that Cleveland's progressive upper-
class women spent their spare dollars and time. The Y
was their "cause." Aunt Cora, the wife of the presi-

dent of a large hardware company, was on the YWCA board. She introduced me to the executive director and president of the board, who suggested I do some volunteer work. I was appointed to the department for industrial women, organizing the young women working in the factories and in low-paying clerical jobs.

Girls came to the YWCA for friendship, especially to meet women from other mills, and to use the gym and swimming pool. The YWCA, however, was determined to give them more than just an escape from the pressures of the workplace. Through a variety of small groups and clubs, young women were encouraged to develop organizing and leadership skills, learn about the responsibilities of citizenship, and the role of women in public affairs. While they could not rise to leadership positions at work or at home, they could become officers in the Y clubs.

I was asked to supervise a club for factory workers called the Hot 'n Tots. It was the first time I ever really got to know women out of my class. While many of them had one dingy dress to their name, I had a closet full at home. I felt guilty and responsible for their plight.

I came up with the idea of having suppers for the girls in the Y cafeteria, to be followed by discussion. I remember the first supper. I was horrified by the girls' table manners. I decided from then on I would teach them the correct way to sit at the table and eat. At the next supper I tried to make subtle comments suggesting that they wait until everyone was served before digging in. I was so pleased with myself and thought they would be forever grateful to me for my advice.

A short time later I began a course in what we called "group work" offered by the YWCA and Western Reserve's School of Social Work. The course focused on class differences, and the professor was a YWCA national staff member, Grace Coyle.

When it was my turn to report on what I was doing in the clubs of working-class women I supervised, I proudly mentioned my attempts to improve their manners. Grace Coyle corrected me. "You are doing these girls a terrible disservice," she said. "You're running the risk of disassociating them from their social class and making it difficult for them to have happy marriages. They will aspire to marry out of their class. Class differences should be respected, not destroyed!"

I took her advice, but I'm still not sure whether she was right. In some ways I thought those young women should be empowered to move out of their limited world.

In the YWCA I met Grace Mayette, a brilliant socialist whom I admired greatly. Mayette was a manly woman with a thick southern drawl who brought obvious conviction to her work as a staff member and secretary in the Industrial Department. Mayette became my mentor for a short time. We used to visit for half an hour every week or so, and she would talk to me about what I was doing and why it was important to organize these young women. She believed in their collective power. I was ready for her ideas.

It was becoming apparent to me that my life was going in a different direction from that of my college classmates. Marge Yarian, my roommate, became engaged during our senior year to a young doctor and polo player. When she married the week after graduation, I was one of her bridesmaids. The couple bought a house in the prosperous suburb of Shaker Heights with lots of ground to keep their horses. Marge began to lead the life that many women of my generation aspired to.

Several times I accompanied Mayette as she went to factories to distribute literature about the YWCA. I remember standing on the floor of a garment factory before what seemed like hundreds—no, thousands—of women bent over sewing machines. Like Mayette, many of my colleagues at the YWCA were socialists, and I joined and became active in the local Young Socialists League. You might say our meetings were an early expression of feminism. While we talked in broad terms of "utopia," capitalism, and the rights of labor, the beneficiaries of most of the reforms we had in mind were women. Until that point, women had been largely excluded from the labor movement.

I never dared mention these meetings to my father though I was full of the subject. After a year as a YWCA volunteer, I was hired as the assistant business and professional "secretary." Y secretaries were the backbone of the organization. They were in charge of the different departments for "industrial" girls, business girls, and for general health and recreation. My first salary was nine hundred dollars a year.

———

During this time I continued to live at home. Sam had graduated from high school and it was expected that he too would go to college. Wooster College, a Presbyterian college that my father approved of, was chosen. Sam enrolled in 1926, the year I graduated. From the beginning, things did not go well.

Sam immediately became homesick and did not find companions. He frequently returned home on weekends. He was at loose ends about exams and term papers. Early on, I offered to help him with his studies. I traveled to Wooster several times for weekend stays. We would pore over his books and notes together. It helped some, but probably not enough. Sam was miserable.

He finished his first year and entered his second year with a little more confidence. However, during the second term of his sophomore year, he had a sort of breakdown. One weekend, while my parents and I were away, Sam returned home and hid in one of the upstairs attic bedrooms. When we returned we did not know he was there. It sickens me today to think of us sitting at dinner, laughing and discussing the day's affairs, while Sam hid upstairs, a refugee in his father's house. He was there for several days, until we discovered him late one night creeping downstairs for food.

Sam refused to return to school and there was nothing we could do to change his mind. He remained in bed for several weeks, despondent and uncommunicative. Our family physician examined him but offered no diagnosis. He prescribed bed rest. In those days little was known about mental illness; it was a family's private grief.

While my mother wanted only to nurse Sam to health, my father was furious and impatient with my brother. He had great plans for Sam—college and then a business career. If Sam had "the will" and applied himself, my father would insist, he could accomplish all this. He could not understand that Sam was intimidated by him and that this approach exacerbated Sam's antisocial behavior.

Every time the issue came to a head, my father would sink into a stony silence that would sometimes last for days. My mother would advise us "to let him be." There weren't battles. People didn't rant and rave at each other in our house. But there was a quiet war going on.

In an attempt to get Sam started at some profession, my father gave him a job at his office doing credit analysis. It was a disaster. My father had exacting standards and Sam did not "measure up." He worked slowly and never completed enough reports on time. The relationship between my father and Sam only grew worse.

One Sunday my parents and I were returning from church without Sam when the issue came up. My mother was driving, and my father was in one of his glum, pouting moods. Nevertheless, I spoke up. I told him I was deeply worried about Sam and felt that he had mistreated him. These were things I had never dared to say before. "I feel I have stolen Sam's birthright," I said. I wept. My father stared straight ahead and said nothing.

CHAPTER 3

Benevolent Ladies

In 1930, when I was twenty-five years old, my father was transferred again, this time to Philadelphia. In the hopes of finding a job with the Young Women's Christian Association there, I traveled to the organization's national convention in Detroit. I remember I wore a smart red coat with a mink collar and hat. I was an earnest young woman, with long chestnut hair wrapped into two little knots in the back of my head.

When I walked into Detroit's Masonic Temple on the first day of the convention and saw the spectacle before me—several thousand women representing what appeared to be every walk of life and every layer of society—I felt part of a great and historic enterprise.

I was interviewed by a Mrs. William Ellis Shipley, a Quaker who was president of the YWCA in the Germantown section of Philadelphia. Across the country YWCA's were started by women like her, the wives of affluent businessmen, doctors, or lawyers who yearned for something they could devote themselves to, something that wasn't frivolous. Mrs. Shipley and I immediately liked each other. I don't remember what we discussed, but we felt a rapport, and I was hired to head the Professional Department of business girls at the YWCA of Germantown. As "business secretary" I would be in charge of programs for Germantown's young "business and professional women"—low-paid secretaries, department store clerks, clerical workers, bookkeepers, and elementary school teachers.

With my new position, any lingering regret over my thwarted teaching career disappeared. I had a job I believed in and threw myself into my work as if there were no tomorrow. Unlike some of my peers, I never thought of my job as "something I'll do until I marry."

The YWCA occupied a four-story brick building in the heart of Germantown's busy commercial district and was a short trolley ride from the apartment house where my parents, Sam, and I lived. I arrived in Germantown during the Depression and the economic base of the area was clearly shifting. The mills that manufactured carpets, textiles, radios, and full-fashioned hosiery were beginning to decline, merge, and move to the South. Many people were thrown out of work and there was no unemployment insurance to cushion them.

Still, there wasn't the same atmosphere of despair that prevails in many urban neighborhoods today. One had the sense that the community remained vital despite the suffering of individuals. This vitality was evident in the lobby and meeting rooms of the YWCA, meticulously furnished and maintained by the organization's patrons.

When I first came to Germantown, I was often called on to chaperone YWCA dances, an awkward assignment given that I was so young myself. It was my responsibility to make sure that the men and women did not leave the auditorium. Naturally many alliances were forged at these dances and the couples liked to go to their cars to get to know each other better. As with my early teaching experience, discipline was not my strong suit and many of my captives escaped.

We may have chaperoned dances and hosted fashion shows, but those of us who worked as Y secretaries thought of ourselves as community activists and social reformers. To be a Y secretary was like running a union and a community center, a church and a social action organization all at once. I was especially zealous about my responsibilities to reach out and organize. I remember sitting in the Horn & Hardart cafeteria at School and Armat lanes in Germantown and striking up conversations with the young women who came in for coffee. I would also go round to offices and department stores and talk to the young women while they worked. I urged the women to come to the Y, if only to use the swimming pool, in the hope that they might then sign up for our Sunday night discussion group, a course in "mental hygiene," or the League of Professional and Business Women. I was constantly recruiting and at the end of each week would tally up how many women I had contacted.

I often tell people that much of my philosophy of life comes from those years with the YWCA, a comment that puzzles people who know the Y only for its swimming pools and aerobics. Today the moral mission of the YWCA has faded, and there is nothing quite like the organization I knew, no group that offers the same combination of services and social action, of conviction and tolerance. I believe the Y was one of the most successful feminist organizations this country ever had.

In Germantown the average job for women paid six dollars, and a "good" job paid ten dollars, for a six-day week. We urged the young women to realize that though they held lowly positions, they had collective strength. We sent many women to the Bryn Mawr Summer School at Bryn Mawr College, where they learned the tactics of unionizing and met union leaders.

The YWCA considered itself a kind of training ground for women, a place for them to begin to become active in women's issues and issues in society. I wanted the women to really *study* their own lives and their place in the world. I remember holding an exhibit of local products at the Y. We sent letters to manufacturers inviting them to send samples of their products. When I returned from a conference a few days later, my desk was piled with swatches of stockings, carpets, and yarn. I got the girls to discuss the products. My, what serious business it was! They talked about "truth in advertising," the profits made in cosmetics and drugs, and the conditions under which many of the products were manufactured. The discussions were carried over by the committee to the social hygiene class, which discussed the role of women as "purchasing agents" for the home.

I started a class on marriage and human sexuality for the women in my department. Quite radical for that time, the class discussed everything from the mechanics of sex to birth control, sexual pleasure, pregnancy, the trials of motherhood, and the difficulties of remaining single in a world where marriage was the norm. The course always filled up quickly and the students, most of them still unmarried, loved it. This was the first time many of these women had ever talked about their bodies!

It is hard to convey today how exciting a national women's organization on the scale of the YWCA was in the '30s and '40s. Remember, men had large trade associations and political parties and clubs long before women. The League of Business and Professional Women in Germantown was related to other leagues in the region, and the regions were brought together nationally in the Business and Professional Council. We were always going off to one conference or another. It seems ordinary now—when so many associations like this hold thousands of conferences every year—but back then it was still a novelty.

I remember traveling with a young clerical worker to a regional conference at Wells College in western New York. It was her first journey outside Philadelphia and her first sight of rolling hills. She made several friends among the delegates and later corresponded with young women from Baltimore, Boston, and Annapolis. She was thrilled to meet women from "so far away" and had long discussions with them about their jobs and family lives. She had been so quiet at meetings at home that I was surprised when she began to pour out all kinds of ideas. The conference had been a releasing experience for her.

My father, Samuel Frederick Kuhn. My mother, Minnie Louise Kooman. AUTHOR'S COLLECTION

My brother, Sam, and I in 1910. I'm five years old. Sam is two. AUTHOR'S COLLECTION

With my Gamma Delta Tau sorority sisters, 1925. I'm in the far-left hand corner. AUTHOR'S COLLECTION

Having fun at the beach at Ocean City, New Jersey, with our YWCA drama group, 1934. AUTHOR'S COLLECTION

At camp Tincicum in Bucks County, Pennsylvania, with my YWCA colleague, Ruth Doud, 1933. AUTHOR'S COLLECTION

On the boardwalk in Atlantic City. I've always been known to wear many hats. AUTHOR'S COLLECTION

On the Johnny Carson show, 1974. NBC PHOTOS

"Age and youth in action"—an anti-nuke demonstration in 1979. Washington, D.C.

At home among the papers.

Jesse Jackson and I close ranks at the 1984 Democratic National Convention in San Francisco.

Claude Pepper and I mixing politics with pleasure at the 1984 Democratic National Convention.

With Dr. Benjamin Spock protesting cuts in healthcare in front of the White House during the Reagan years, 1986.

With my cat, Charlotte Brontë. © I. GEORGE BILYK. ALL

My "family of choice" sitting on the porch steps of my house in Germantown, 1981. © *Philadelphia Inquirier*/SHARON WOHLMUTH

For many years, YWCA secretaries received training in New York City at YWCA headquarters. In the spring of 1929 I enrolled and went to live in New York for several months. If I had been a student some twenty years before, I would have had a different kind of schooling. One class member of 1911 told Marion O. Robinson, author of *Eight Women of the YWCA*, that she was taught, among other things, that when visiting in a board member's home, she must "never put out combs and brushes on the bedroom dresser without first slipping a piece of tissue paper underneath."

By the time I arrived the training was less like finishing school and more like graduate school. Along with our courses at YWCA headquarters, we took courses in social work and theology at Columbia University's Teachers College and Union Theological Seminary. We met some of the leading thinkers and social reformers of the day. I will never forget my class with Harry Emerson Fosdick, by then the renowned pastor of Riverside Presbyterian Church. Fosdick's theories on Christian activism were an extension of what I had learned in my Bible literature course in college. Every generation should interpret the Bible anew, he said, and apply its meaning to the great issues of the day. Nor will I forget the renowned philosopher and theologian Reinhold Niebuhr, a tall, gangly man who ran his hand through his sparse hair as he talked to us of the "relentless forces of history."

In those years the YWCA thought of itself as a Christian organization that served both Christians and non-Christians alike. It did not proselytize, as did the YWCA's founders, ladies who ventured into factories in the early 1800s carrying portable organs and hymnbooks. These early crusaders visited bakeries and cigar factories in Pittsburgh, paper mills in Kalamazoo, cotton mills in South Carolina, and department stores in San Francisco in the hope of offering spiritual sustenance to the new class of working women that had sprung up around the country.

However, from early on, some of the ladies were not content simply to seek converts. In 1859 Lucretia Boyd, the founder of the first Young Women's Christian Association in this country, decried the plight of the working girl: "The majority live in attic rooms of lodging houses, struggling with poverty, loneliness, and isolation; neglected in sickness, helpless when out of work and subject to chance acquaintance from the lower strata of society. Cannot something be done by benevolent ladies?"

Indeed, the Y's founders discovered that the workers had little thought of a world beyond this one, so caught up were they in the miserable struggles of their lives. According to Germantown legend, a Quaker woman went to a garment mill at lunchtime and preached to the girls working there about vanity. She pointed out that the dress she was wearing was fifteen years old. After a pause one of the girls, a silk spinner, spoke up: "Yes, but if everyone wore their clothes that long there would be no work for us." To which the Quaker woman replied, "Thee has given me a new idea."

In the twentieth century the YWCA became the foremost advocate for working women. Disturbed by the lack of decent housing for young working women, YWCA's established hundreds of affordable residences. They started the first typing classes, the first school for nurses, the first day nursery. Immigrants flowing into the country's harbors were met by women working for the YWCA. Later the Y would encourage women to join unions and would support legislation that would improve their working conditions.

Initally a loose confederation of city associations and student groups, the YWCA became a single organization in December 1906 under the leadership of Grace Dodge, the first national president. Six feet tall, reserved, and brilliant, Dodge was the unmarried daughter of William E. Dodge, Jr., of the wealthy New York family. I would love to have known her. Bringing her family's legendary business acumen to her social works and philanthropy, she helped build the Y into an international movement. "Our movement is going to live for centuries," she said in 1909. "We have to look at what thousands of girls will want or need in the future."

Many, though not all, of the YWCA's early leaders were unmarried and they zealously devoted themselves to the organization. They were courageous, shrewd, and determined, and the absence of their names from our history books is an indication of how undervalued are women's achievements. Mabel Cratty, an unmarried schoolteacher from Delaware,

Ohio, was the national YWCA's first general secretary, a post she held for twenty-two years. During Cratty's tenure from 1906 to 1928, the organization's budget grew from $136,000 to more than $2 million and the membership of its national board from fourteen to one hundred and one. Like the Y women of her generation, she combined deep religious feeling with the desire for social reform.

It was the extraordinary alliance between upper- and lower-class women that gave the YWCA its strength. I think the wealthy women were motivated partly by noblesse oblige, but there was also a genuine compassion for working women. As a delegate from Illinois at the organization's 1920 convention asked, "Do we as Christian women really want other women to work nights and seven days a week so that we may have more leisure and more things?"

The issues debated and resolved at that convention in Cleveland set the tone for the organization I later worked for. Deciding to take a more active role in defending the working woman, the Y adopted the Social Ideals of the Churches, a controversial social platform that had been adopted by the Federal Council of Churches in 1912. The Ideals, among other things, stated that women "should have full political and economic equality with equal pay for equal work, and a maximum eight-hour day."

According to records of the convention, one national board member urged defeat of the platform, stating, "My fear has been that on account of the trend of our time toward radical socialism, a trend which I regret to say I have found even in certain departments of our association that we love so much, that we may be caught up in a current that will lead us into very unfortunate conditions." Many of the ladies who voted in favor of the measure were said to have met angry husbands when they returned home from the convention.

In Germantown my work also brought the Y's affluent benefactresses and working-class members together. Keen on offering the members the sort of intellectual stimulation they could not find at work, I revived the practice of Sunday night discussion groups, where small groups of men and women would meet in board members' homes to discuss the issues of the day. We usually met in one of the stone mansions in Mount Airy. Our deep dark purpose was to become a force in creating public support for workplace reform and industrial democracy. Such lofty ambitions!

I remember one Sunday when we were sitting around drinking tea and discussing controversial sit-down strikes by the country's factory workers. Just that week, striking workers had been arrested. Suddenly, during our discussion, a small, elderly Quaker woman stood up and shook her fist. "That's what we need," she said, "more brushes with the police!"

Sometimes distinguished speakers were invited to attend. There were heated discussions with the former French consul who spoke about the fall of the French republic. He had nothing but scorn for the pacifists in France and England, and warned against the peace movement in the United States as well. There were also tense, impassioned debates about one Germantown resident's presentation of Nazi Germany. He had just returned from two years in Germany and tried to relate what the Nazis were attempting to do in Germany for the workers, the farmers, and the youth groups. Many members of the group thought him a Nazi sympathizer. Two, however, agreed with him most heartily because they said they believed that Hitler had accomplished a great deal and that England was never to be trusted.

I invited several members of the YWCA's black branch to attend these discussions. Though the Y had long spoken out in favor of equal rights for blacks, the associations were still segregated. Germantown had large numbers of Italian and Irish, who lived in separate neighborhoods and attended different Catholic churches, and there was open discrimination against blacks. I'll never forget some of the stories our friends from the Y's black branch told us. One man who "passed" for white was able to purchase a house in a white neighborhood, but he had his family use the back door to keep their presence quiet. He had been hired as an office manager at one of the big Center City firms and was doing well. Then one day his son, who was dark skinned, showed up at the office to ask his father for money to go to the movies. The next day the man was dismissed from his job.

One of the things I valued most about the Y was its belief in the ability of groups to empower the individual and to change society. Social workers back then called it "group work." The idea was that individuals find purpose and meaning through group association.

As Y secretaries, we were taught not to interfere with the democratic process but to allow people to learn how to govern groups that could arrive at decisions themselves. Our ideals often took a beating.

One of the activities I started was the Play Shop, an amateur theater group of men and women inspired by the Group Theater in New York City. Our Play Shop was meant to be an experiment in democracy with everyone participating in major decisions about each production. We wanted plays with serious social content. However, the young director, a local talent we had begged to come and work with us, was dictatorial and insisted on choosing the plays himself. One meeting ended in a free-for-all when the director tried to force his favorite play upon the group. The director's best friend rose and called him names, whereupon he, who always had a fine feeling for the dramatic, stalked out of the room. The meeting broke up into excited factions.

Though the Y was a women's organization, I often tried to involve men in our activities since so many young women were anxious to meet suitors. On one occasion, in 1938, we invited a group of YMCA men to a steak roast hosted by the League. It was to be a gracious affair, with intelligent conversation on business and current events. Two carloads of raucous YMCA men responded to the invitation. They proceeded to set up a miniature traveling bar in one of the cars. For the next get-together, I went to the other extreme and invited a group of Lutheran seminarians.

While I worked at the Y, I started to date Ernest Bennett, the son of a Delaware River tugboat captain. Lovable and easygoing, he had no great passions in life. I think I liked him because he was so different from me, less serious and driven. Unemployed when I met him, as were many men in those Depression years, he finally landed a job selling life insurance and joked that he was "a human engineer." Ernest was a good dancer, and we used to fox-trot and waltz at the dances held in the rooftop ballroom at the Mayfair House. We were both living with our parents so we had to improvise venues for lovemaking. In the wintertime we used his car. In the summer and fall, we would stretch out on a blanket under the stars and the azalea bushes in Fairmount Park. It was uncomfortable but romantic.

Ernest was subject to particularly harsh treatment by my father who refused to speak to my friend even when they were in the same room. My father would sit there reading his newspaper or book as if Ernest had never appeared. It was embarrassing and rude. My mother and I were very distressed by it.

I asked my father why he so strenuously objected to Ernest. "He's not good enough for you," he responded curtly. Nevertheless, I dated Ernest for several years. Marriage was never considered because Ernest could barely support himself. Besides, though we had some great times, we were not soulmates.

At that time my parents, Sam, and I lived on the eighth floor of the Mayfair House, a fashionable high-rise apartment building on Lincoln Drive overlooking the Wissahickon Valley. From our windows we could see the owner of the Phillies, Connie Mack, walk his dog in his garden. By this time my father had made several real estate investments in Cleveland and, during the economic collapse of 1929, lost a great deal of money. He had soured on real estate and vowed he would never buy another house.

Sam had found a job doing credit reporting for a small company that allowed him to work out of the house. He liked the work and the company seemed pleased with him. But there was more bizarre behavior. One day I came home and found Sam standing in the hallway of our apartment. He was wearing one of my strapless evening dresses, stretched tight around his hulking frame. "Sam! What are you doing?" I cried. Stricken with embarrassment, he rushed into his bedroom and slammed the door shut.

Later I found the dress in my room, ripped beyond repair. It would be the first of many dresses he would ruin. I was extremely upset. What was Sam doing? What was going on in his mind? I did not dare discuss the matter with my brother or my parents or anyone. I thought about it long and hard. I didn't read sexual motives into Sam's behavior, but came to the conclusion that he tried on my clothes because he wanted to be me. I was the perfect daughter. He was the son who could do nothing right. In being good and in being happy, I had brought torment to my brother. I was deeply ashamed of the contrast between us.

Though Sam had been a lovely boy, whom my mother dressed in stylish knickers and jackets, he had become an ungainly man. Short and overweight, he was too big for his clothes. Outside of a few acquaintances he had met at church, he had no friends.

Within a few years it became clear that Sam was mentally ill. Gradually, he had withdrawn further and further into his own world. The apartments in our building were situated so that you could look from our window into apartments across the courtyard. Sam would stand at our living room window, sometimes all day and night, and stare with a frightening intensity into other people's apartments.

This voyeurism horrified my father, who would shout across the room, "Sam, stop that! Get away from the window at once!" Sam would react like a wounded animal, slinking away to his room only to resume his place at the window later.

My father was extremely upset about Sam's deterioration, but he wouldn't talk about it with my mother or me. The more upset he was, the quieter he became. I believe that deep inside he was not angry with Sam anymore but tormented with uncertainty about what to do to help him. Both my parents felt confused. So little was known and openly discussed in those days about mental illness. I sensed that my mother blamed my father for having pushed Sam beyond his limits. Several times my mother and I sat down with Sam and gently begged him to see a psychiatrist. Sam would rave, shouting, "I won't go! I won't go!" It seemed there was nothing more we could do.

Much of this is painful to remember. I became so adept at blocking it out that today when I look back on it, I can't recall many of the details. It's a blur. I remember meditating in moments alone, repeating the same phrases over and over: "Give me patience, Lord. Give me strength, Lord, and endurance."

To escape the pressure, I would take a box of watercolors and paper to quiet spots along Wissahickon Creek not far from our apartment building. The Wissahickon Valley in Fairmount Park has beautiful ravines and forested paths. When I painted, I would think of nothing but the scene before me. It was a great form of therapy. When I look at the watercolors I have saved from then I don't remember the difficulties, only a sense of inner peace.

In 1938 my mother became ill with a kidney infection and was hospitalized for a month at Women's Medical College. Her doctor, a woman, came to know our family well. She immediately sensed that something was wrong with Sam, who visited my mother often in the hospital, and drew the entire story from my mother. When my mother's health had improved and she was ready to go home, the doctor came to my mother's room and said, "I'm not going to discharge you until you do something about your son." She insisted that Sam be hospitalized.

Ten years earlier this step would have been inconceivable to us. But Sam had changed so profoundly. We were relieved the doctor had made the decision for us. My father took the initiative and arranged to have Sam admitted to Norristown State Hospital, about a twenty-minute drive from our home. In those days committing a person to a mental hospital was easier than it is today. Only one physician's signature and my father's consent were required. A hospital attendant arrived at our apartment one morning to take Sam away. To our surprise, he went willingly. In fact, it went so smoothly that I wondered if Sam wasn't as relieved as we were.

Norristown was a progressive hospital, not just a warehouse for the insane. It was run by Dr. Arthur Noyes, an outstanding psychiatrist who became a pioneer in the field by making Norristown one of the first institutions to open doors of patients' buildings so that many of them could walk freely about the grounds. The emphasis was on group therapy and rehabilitation. Many of the patients were given jobs working in the hospital's cafeteria, pharmacy, and farm fields. The fruits and vegetables grown in the fields were served in the cafeteria.

Sam, who had a room of his own, seemed to like the place immediately. But I didn't know much about his life there. For the first few years that Sam was in the hospital, I seldom went to Norristown. My mother and I decided not to go visit Sam for a while so that my father would take responsibility for his role in my brother's life. We both recognized that there would be no healing in this situation unless my brother and father resolved their conflicts and were reconciled. My father visited Sam faithfully once a week. It was obvious from the things he said when he came home that he had begun to have compassion for Sam and to accept him.

CHAPTER 4

The Homefront

Many people ask why I never married. My glib response is always "Sheer luck!" When I look back on my life, I see so many things I could not have done if I had been tied to a husband and children. Whenever a staff member at the YWCA became engaged to marry, immediate plans were made for her resignation. I remember one young woman, a friend of mine, who worked at the Y as a volunteer. She was married and was having some difficulty getting pregnant. When she went to a doctor for advice, he attributed her infertility to the many hours she spent in gainful activity at the Y. "Spend more time at home," he admonished her, "and then you'll get pregnant."

By the time I reached the age of thirty-five I had come close to marriage twice. The first time was with Paul Foulkes in college. A few years later I almost took the plunge with Paul Southgate, a young doctor in Cleveland, whom I met at Lakeside Hospital when he removed my mother's tonsils. He was charming and handsome. We were attracted to each other in the hospital—not the most conventional setting for a romance—and after my mother left, Paul called the house on the pretense of checking up on her health.

That was the beginning of a heavy-duty love affair.

Paul was the one man whom my father showed a small degree of warmth toward, possibly because they were similar in personality, both driving and domineering. Although we weren't officially engaged, we both assumed marriage was the next step. Paul was planning to set up a practice in Lewistown, Montana, and he came to our house shortly before he left and asked me to come with him. We agreed that I would first visit him and then follow at some indefinite later date.

I took a train out to Lewistown—and loathed it. I absolutely couldn't see myself leaving a career I loved to lead the life of a dutiful doctor's wife in rural Montana. Besides, during the visit, I saw a side of Paul I didn't like. Whenever we went out, he took it upon himself to tell me which dress and hat to wear. How dare he! I took the train home to Cleveland and never looked back.

We regularly held courses at the Y that included discussion on the art—or should I say science?—of marrying and staying married. One popular course was given by Dr. Clara Schoonmaker, a WPA worker supposedly expert in the psychology of sexual relations. "We must be careful about colors!" Dr. Schoonmaker told the young women, who listened with rapt attention. "We often wear colors that are bad for our own and our companion's state of mind. We must learn what colors are suitable for twentieth-century activities!" She advised young married women to wear makeup even at breakfast, so precarious was their hold on the twentieth-century male.

I had always found attracting men easy, almost effortless. I enjoyed male companionship immensely and felt free to enjoy sex. But I had an independent streak. I didn't need a man in my life all the time. I enjoyed a good love affair, but when it was over I was never devastated by the breakup. Salacious as it may sound, I always thought—on to the next!

When I entered my thirties, people began to worry about me. That was around the age when a single woman began to be referred to as a spinster. My mother's friends frequently asked her when I was going to marry. I started to feel the pressure and also, at times, was a little depressed and uncertain about my future. But I didn't dwell on it—nor did I rush out to find a mate.

Like most unmarried women in those days, I lived at home. The responsibilities of taking care of my parents and my brother greatly influenced the course of my life. I felt I was needed at home. But I was not prepared to give up the one part of my life that was all my own—my work.

While the parents of my friends looked forward to the day when their daughters would be married off, my parents never discussed the subject. I think my mother would have liked me to marry, but she didn't want to interfere and liked having me at home. My father, who believed that none of the men I brought home were good enough, was clearly opposed to the idea. I sensed he was actually jealous of my beaus and couldn't bear the idea of sharing me. His attitude angered me deeply, but I didn't cower before his opinion. If I had really wanted to marry, I would have.

In 1941, when I was thirty-six, Sam was adjusting well to Norristown and I felt freer to leave my parents. As the United States prepared to enter World War II, the National Board of the YWCA asked me to come and work in their headquarters in New York City. Here was my chance.

Earlier that year the United Services Organization was formed as the principal civilian agency to assist the Department of Defense in the war effort. The USO was a coalition of six social service organizations: the YWCA, the Young Men's Christian Association, the National Catholic Community Service, the Salvation Army, the Jewish Welfare Board, and the National Travelers Aid. Together, these groups were in charge of many of the daily needs of the troops and their families, looking after their spiritual, recreational, and social welfare. I was recruited to be a program coordinator and editor for the YWCA's USO division.

The USO is well known for its canteens and parties, for passing out coffee and doughnuts to soldiers and sailors, for helping the men get letters home, for Bob Hope and Joey Heatherton. Many remember those famous USO dances. Big army trucks would pick up war workers at their jobs and take them to barracks that served as dance halls. But the USO's mission was broader and deeper. We provided "normalizing influences" in a time when nothing was normal. We were the guardians of civilian morale—and when spirits were down in towns across the country, we succeeded in preserving it. I sometimes wonder what would have happened if the Y and the other agencies in the USO hadn't done what they did. We were a mediating and humanizing force in situations that were horrific, providing a crucial sense of stability in communities where everyday life was turned upside down to accommodate the production of weapons and the training of men.

In the crisis of war, the basic needs of human beings often go unserved. Although I never crossed the Atlantic Ocean or entered enemy territory, I felt close to the war and its frantic pace. The history books focus on the conditions of the soldier, on the battles and the intrigue, on the tactics of army generals and commanders. My concern was with the thousands of smaller dramas at home and, in particular, the huge toll the war took on women.

In our office in New York, we received reports daily from USO centers that served both the spouses of fighting men and women war workers. The reports spoke of loneliness, fatigue, indebtedness—and tremendous fortitude. "Attendance at classes has held up in spite of these difficult days," wrote one West Coast club. "One Tuesday night after war was declared, twenty nurses came to Spanish class. They came early to hear the President's speech and stayed on for the class. One could almost see them force themselves to concentrate. . . . The instructor's fiancé had left with his regiment only that day, but she taught the class."

"Our USO center is working with 125 young women whose husbands were killed in action at Pearl Harbor," read another report. "Many are in desperate need of friendship, sympathy, jobs, personal counseling, help with family problems."

As I traveled around the country to coordinate USO programs, I was awestruck by the changes in the countryside, particularly in the South. Huge military camps and defense plants seemed to spring up overnight in fields of sugar beets and corn. I will never forget those boom times in the small towns of North and South Carolina.

From the start the YWCA saw itself as the advocate of the hundreds of thousands of women recruited to work in defense production plants—continuing the role it had taken on in World War I when it established industrial war work centers. The YWCA recognized that women defense workers—the Rosie the Riveters of the country—were in need of special attention and assistance.

At the onset of war, weapons manufacturers had launched great advertising campaigns for women war workers, appealing to the patriotic duty of homemakers and glamorizing war work. The response was tremendous. In my first year with the USO, over a million women workers had joined the defense industry; by August 1942, 1.75 million women were working in war plants. I remember a poem in the New York *Herald Tribune*:

> Oh, the girl I adore
> Isn't here anymore—

She's a welder at Plant 23.
She works night and day
Getting overtime pay
and she hasn't a moment for me.

In vain do I wait
By the factory gate,
And waiting, I plaintively pine
for a vine-covered porch,
an acetylene torch,
and that little spot-welder of mine.

Scores of young women took to the roads, many of them hitchhiking to defense industry towns. Some arrived before construction of a war plant was complete and the jobs advertised were not yet open. These women often became the temporary wards of the YWCA. It was up to our USO units to house them and then get them home or provide for them until they were employed.

The common view today is that women's liberation benefited from World War II. Hired by defense industries to build aircraft and guns, women found a new freedom and earning power—so the story goes. Those of us working at the YWCA knew that the war had created crushing problems for women. I will never forget the laundresses at a defense camp in Jacksonville, Florida, who slept on the ground in the woods because no housing was made for them; or the women war workers who handled chemicals that made their hair fall out or who packed ammunition that exploded. Drawn by the glamour of military uni-

forms, teenage girls drifted into camp areas, and
women war workers stood in long lines at food stores,
coping with rationing after working a ten-hour shift.
Navy wives made homes for their families in overcrowded trailer camps, struggling to raise their children alone.

Though many believe that women war workers
were middle-class homemakers who responded out of
a sense of duty, I often met workers who were young
girls in their first jobs or who were wives of soldiers
trying to make up for lost income. They desperately
needed the jobs. Wages at the defense plants often
failed to live up to their billing. In 1941 the average
woman in a defense job made less than twenty dollars
a week. Women who made fifteen dollars a week often
spent six dollars to nine dollars a week to rent a room.

Some women could not locate decent housing at
any price. I was appalled to find workers sleeping in
shanties and makeshift dorms with poor cooking
facilities. Four and five workers would share a single
room. Women who worked different shifts often
teamed up to rent a single bed. While one was at work,
the other slept. We called it the "hot bed," because
the sheets never had a chance to cool.

In some towns women had to walk two miles or
more along desolate country roads to and from work,
even when their shifts ended after midnight. Their
dorms were often miles away from the nearest place to
eat. In one midwestern town, where there was no public transportation between the town and dormitories
one and a half miles away, USO workers helped out

one night a week by taking food to the girls who finished work at midnight. Too tired for a recreational program, the girls ate in silence and then went to bed. Many women war workers became unnerved and exhausted. Some simply gave up their jobs and went home.

Inadequate child care was a constant problem. In one New England town, two hundred married women registered in an employment office refused to take work in war industries because they had no place to leave their children. Around the country women were forced into inadequate arrangements for child care, sometimes leaving young children alone. The Y worked hard to help these women find solutions.

Despite all of these problems, the Y had to fight for the opportunity to serve working women and often felt like an outsider in the male-dominated USO. In 1942 the YWCA sent a proposal to Chester Bernard, president of the USO Council, for a program of special services to women war production workers. It proposed that trained YWCA staff work with community leaders in defense towns to mobilize community resources and reorganize programs for female war production workers. According to the proposal:

Women and girls whose entire previous experience has been in the home, on the farm, or in the school, find it difficult to adjust to the speed and strain of war production. . . . [They face] bad living conditions, unfamiliar surroundings, lack of wholesome recreation and normal social relations. These are common to all war production communities and add to the usual problems of health and emotional balance. . . . All of these factors have created in communities, which might normally carry their load of social responsibility, such overwhelming problems that even those which are well organized and possessed of fairly adequate facilities are facing serious problems of readjustment and reorganization of existing facilities and resources.

But many considered the needs of women negligible when compared to the problems of the soldier in the field. Bernard's response indicated how deep this attitude ran. "I do not see any basis, except convenience and expediency, for limiting our consideration to a particular group," he said. As if convenience and expediency weren't enough! Further, he stated,

It seems clear to me that while there is work with women that only women can do and work with men that only men can do, there is also work with men and women which both men and women can do, and there is some work, with men at least, that women can do better than men. . . . My only point in stating these things is to emphasize my opinion that we are proceeding along false lines when we make the fundamentals of our organization dependent upon the sex either of those who are to be benefitted or of those who are to do the work.

Despite Bernard's opposition, the YWCA's plan was accepted. By 1944 there were 244 regional YWCA-USO workers and 97 on the administrative staff at USO headquarters.

The regional workers were our troubleshooters. Ruth Doud, my co-worker in Germantown, was assigned to Dublin, Virginia, home to 150 families until thousands of war workers descended upon it. The workers, many of whom were women, slept anyplace they could find—in garages, over stores, in chicken houses with no plumbing. When there was no place left, they sat along the street curbs all night. Off hours, they aimlessly roamed the streets, overwhelming the town's one drug store, one restaurant, one movie theater.

Doud found families to take in women war workers and persuaded the community to construct sheds for temporary shelter. She worked with the local school to accommodate the overflow of new pupils and found medical care for the newcomers in a town where the only physician had retired ten years before. She converted a storeroom over a grocery to the USO clubroom. "Food and shelter are important," she was quoted as saying in *Life* magazine, "but, goodness, so is fun." She instituted Friday night square dances and Saturday nights of parlor rope tricks.

Recreation *was* an important part of the USO. The

USO centers held thousands of dances and other relaxing diversions and offered classes in such subjects as art and foreign languages. Make no mistake about it: sometimes the organization lived up to its nickname, "Unlimited Sexual Opportunities."

The special problems of wives, mothers, and girlfriends of men in the armed forces were also under the Y's purview. The army and navy men's wives who moved into camp areas often were lonely and at a loss as to how to fill their long, empty hours. Many had picked up stakes to follow their men to training camps and bases. Some were barely out of their teens. They were plagued by what we called "baby and budget troubles."

If they were lucky, navy families lived in barracks, which were often miles from schools, churches, and shopping centers. When the government units were full, the families had to take whatever quarters they could find. I remember visiting one family of four in their basement room. There was a seething frustration among many of the women. One navy wife wrote in one of our USO newsletters:

No woman who has lived in the same city all her life, who has had her husband home every night, who has been a respected member of her community can begin to understand the world of a transient. Years of discrimination and ostracism have taught the sailor's wife that she is not part of civic life, that she must stick to her own in self-defense. . . . Since the outbreak of hostilities, I have lived in six defense centers, all of them presenting the same problems of congestion, high rents, inadequate recreation. But welfare boards and defense councils do not like us to complain about their towns. . . . I, as a Navy wife, don't want to feel that my morale must be kept high; I want to belong. I want to be an integral part of the city where I make my home.

I remember seeing the wives of defense workers scrubbing their clothes in buckets and tubs in a squalid trailer camp. They usually made their homes in camps like that at the edge of a town or in dingy "rooms for light housekeeping."

There was often extraordinary tension between the transients and residents in the boom towns. You can imagine a sleepy town of three thousand being inundated by a camp of ninety thousand. On weekends soldiers and defense workers, whom we called "men on the loose," might become drunk and disorderly. Civilians often resented the strangers simply because their sheer numbers had so altered life in the towns. Local residents frequently exploited the newcomers by raising housing prices. Greed was not checked by patriotism.

We held social gatherings to introduce newcomers and residents, and to try to smooth over conflict. Y volunteers would visit the homes and trailers of the newcomers. In one USO center, the townspeople arranged weekly square-dancing parties, making it a rule that every resident come with a newcomer.

Many of those North and South Carolina towns were strictly Protestant and had never known Catholics and Jews. The Sunday before the opening of maneuvers in one North Carolina town, our USO unit arranged to have the first Catholic mass celebrated there in 156 years. It was arranged by the USO and held in the movie house. Would the town have been so accommodating without us?

Those years taught me a great deal about conflict, about living with it and not being overcome by it. I was amazed when I traveled in the South and witnessed the tension between blacks and whites. Here we were one nation struggling against fascism, and our own troops were segregated, with blacks clearly the outcasts. When I went to represent the YWCA in a USO Council meeting in Charleston, I was shocked to see the black members standing in the back of the room; they were not permitted to sit down!

President Roosevelt, in his Columbus Day speech in 1942, addressed the issue: "In some communities, employers dislike to hire women. In others, they are reluctant to hire Negroes. We can no longer afford to indulge such prejudice."

The YWCA held itself up as a watchdog against discrimination. "Actions which are not only un-Christlike but definitely harmful to the individuals concerned and to our country are being brought to our attention daily," said Mary Ingraham, then president of the YWCA National Board who had publicly protested the statement by the president of a large aircraft factory that "under no circumstances will Negroes be employed as aircraft workers or mechanics."

In Wichita, Kansas, the Interracial Committee of the YWCA established an interracial commission that protested the barring of Negroes from local defense training centers. One large city in the South had no recreational facilities for its large population of black families. When blacks poured into camps in and around the city, they had no place to go in their off-hours. Prodded by USO workers, the mayor appointed the city's first interracial committee. It designed and built the town's first recreation facilities for blacks.

I traveled a fair amount in those days, visiting USO units to make them feel part of the USO empire. Those of us who worked for the USO would have liked to have traveled more, but the military had priority on the trains. When non-military traveled by train, it was rare that you could get a berth; four people would be packed in one coach seat with all their luggage! The little luxuries of train travel had disappeared. There were no longer flowers on the tables in the dining cars.

Our office was in a little annex to the YWCA building at 600 Lexington Avenue, an elegant white fieldstone structure built with the large sums donated by Grace Dodge. I'll never forget the simple engraving in the marble entry hall: "To the Glory of God in

Service for Young Women this building is dedicated in the year of our Lord 1912."

The building had a homey touch despite all the important business carried on there. Beyond its huge vaulted central hall with polished terrazzo floors there were welcoming sitting rooms and offices with antique furnishings. There was an assembly room with glittering chandeliers, five balconies, and rococo decor. Every Thursday the entire staff would gather for tea in a lounge on the fifth floor, where we would sit on antique chairs given by wealthy board members.

I liked being at the heart of the organization I had worked for for so long. People like Abby Rockefeller and Mary French, prominent members of the YWCA National Board, walked the same hallways. I marveled at the deep commitment of those wealthy matrons.

I met many inspiring women during my years at the Y. There was a quality about them—an inner strength, a spirit of independence, a brand of determination—that I have drawn from all my life.

I had the privilege of working with Rhoda McCullough, the editor of the *Women's Press*, the YWCA's national magazine. She was a brilliant writer and thinker who wore manly suits and never powdered her nose or carried a lipstick. Before she entered a meeting, she would take two military brushes from her desk and flatten her short-cropped hair with two brisk strokes.

In the 1920s and '30s, McCullough wrote essays that captured the spirit of the organization. "The Young Women's Christian Association believes in [a] philosophy of the wholeness of life," she wrote. "Its educational programs are built to produce in a community not a crop of glib, easily spoken opinions; its chief product is character." McCullough invited me to write for the *Women's Press*, and I sought her help with the many USO bulletins and newsletters I would edit. She used to call me "My dear."

All of the women on the USO/YWCA staff were unmarried and hardworking. I remember the clouds of cigarette smoke that hung over the desks and filled the meeting rooms. There was a great esprit de corps among us. A favorite saying in the office was "To get along in a man's world you have to look like a school-girl, dress like a lady, think like a man, and work like a horse."

Genevieve Lowry, a woman in her fifties whom we called Aunt Gen, was director of the YWCA's USO Division. Like McCullough, she was masculine in appearance, with short dark hair and well-tailored suits. She was an exceptional, physically imposing woman, almost six feet tall and always the biggest person in the room. Lowry had started with the Y as an industrial secretary in St. Joseph, Missouri, and had headed the YWCA's foreign divisions in Hangchow, China, and Istanbul.

It was common knowledge that some of the women at the Y were lesbian and lived with their lovers. It was not a subject of discussion, only quiet acceptance. I, on the other hand, had a reputation for being a real snake charmer with men. My co-workers would always say teasingly, "Maggie has *no* trouble getting dates."

Some YWCA staff and board members were am-

bivalent about the war and questioned our involvement in the USO. The organization included many
women who were pacifists on religious grounds. Since
the government had asked all groups to suspend national meetings, we never had a chance to wrestle with
the issue at a national convention. Those of us in the
USO division were truly part of the war effort and
could not question it too deeply. I remember when my
assistant Mary Tobin returned from a trip visiting
USO centers around the country. She was buoyed by
the spirit at military camps and defense plants. "For
the first time, I think we're really going to win this
war," she told us during a meeting. We all stood up
and clapped.

It seemed as though we had gobs of money at our
disposal. With all their flag-waving fanfare, the USO
fund-raising campaigns were enormously successful;
we had larger budgets than we had ever dreamed possible at the YWCA. Gen would tell our staff, "For
heaven's sake, spend it!"

When I first came to New York, I stayed in the
YWCA residence at the "600" building. My room
had a sink, a humble closet, and a view of the magnificent city around us. I was just an elevator ride away
from my office.

I eventually rented an apartment for eighty-five
dollars a month at 340 East 52nd Street and found a
roommate, Kay Catterns, a charming and intelligent
British woman who came to this country to work on
a defense project for the British Library of Information. Kay and I became fast friends. We liked living

together. A trained librarian, Kay was more organized than me, and she would sometimes complain about my work papers stacked about the apartment. She called me "Maggie Bottleneck."

It was impossible to get a hotel room in New York during the war, so many of Kay's friends took us up on our open-door policy. On any given night there was sure to be someone from the British Empire on our pull-out couch.

I loved walking the few blocks back and forth from the office to our brownstone. I got to know the butcher, the pharmacist, and the other vendors along the route. We would always exchange the latest news and worries about the war. During rationing, I could always count on the butcher to reserve a lamb chop or two for me in his cooler. On the nights when the city's lights were blacked out to prevent attack, I was glad my commute was so short.

When I had a chance, I loved going to one of the city's exotic restaurants. Back then a Chinese restaurant was such a novelty to me. I would always wear a fancy hat when I was out on the town, and to this day, I have a closet full of headgear that attests to my dashing appearance back then. I remember one evening that I spent in a restaurant in Greenwich Village with some co-workers. I was wearing a little velvet beret with a decorative bird pinned to the front. I had taken such care in finding just the right bird for the hat. When the waiter opened a bottle of champagne for the table next to ours, the cork shot up like a missile and hit my bird, which fell with a plop into my soup.

Under normal circumstances, New York City may be the most exciting place in the world for a single person to live, but I was there at a trying time. The war imposed curfews and restraint on a city known for its high life. Although I had friends who danced and drank the night away every night, career took precedence for me. I got a great deal of satisfaction from doing my job well. A good love affair requires a certain amount of time, and some nights must be sacrificed. I usually needed those nights to meet a deadline.

It had been hard for my parents to accept my going to New York. They were outwardly gracious about it, but their faces showed the strain. By the time I left, my mother was seventy-four and my father seventy-one. I returned home frequently for weekends and we would sometimes spend Sunday visiting Sam at Norristown. It was clear that Sam was thriving. He had a girlfriend—among the patients—a job he liked in the hospital's pharmacy, and friends.

Finally the war ended. I barely remember celebrating. With the signing of the armistice, our work at the USO quadrupled. As Aunt Gen was quoted as saying in the New York *World Telegram*, "In a way, [it is like] something a Sunday school teacher once said: 'The most disconcerting thing about prayer is when it's answered.' The sudden end of the war, for which we all prayed, found us quite unprepared."

As war work came to a halt, there were massive layoffs of women, everyone from assembly line workers to teachers and college professors. Men had been promised their jobs would be waiting when they returned. Attendance at USO clubs soared as women turned to us for counseling and information on unemployment insurance and job opportunities. We organized all-day job fairs and rushed in field-workers to meet with the unemployed. Many women resigned themselves to accepting lower-paid jobs, while others turned to traditional roles as wives and mothers.

In those years I worked so hard my health suffered. During one period of intensive travel, I contracted a bad sinus infection that brought headaches, a runny nose, and a raspy throat. I went to a throat specialist who prescribed a treatment of Argyrol. I sat for several sessions in the doctor's office, my nose packed with cotton wads soaked in Argyrol. The medicine seeps into the subcutaneous layers of the skin and clears the sinuses. I was too impatient to finish the treatment at the doctor's office and decided to administer the rest of the Argyrol to myself at home at night. What a mistake.

One morning I woke up and gasped when I looked in the mirror. I was a silvery gray color. I looked like a corpse. When I went to the office, the faces of my co-workers registered their disbelief. "What happened to you? Look at your face!" They said. I burst into tears.

I immediately went to another doctor, who put me in the hospital. I was Exhibit A; the doctors had never seen such an advanced case of Argyrolosis. There was little they could do to revive my former coloring. I went to a beauty clinic after I left the hospital and they prescribed a powder to hide my pallor. But even with the makeup, people thought I was on the verge of a heart attack. To this day I have my silver lining—a souvenir of the war.

CHAPTER 5

Hunting Buffalo

When my father first arrived in Philadelphia in 1929, he would walk the four blocks from the Warwick Hotel, the elegant downtown hotel where he was staying, to First Presbyterian Church on Twenty-first Street. He was seeking familiar terrain, like a bird who has migrated many hundreds of miles to nest in the same sort of marshy grass or high tree he left behind. First Presbyterian was the closest thing there was to Old Stone, our church in Cleveland.

One of the oldest and most prominent Presbyterian congregations in this country, First Presbyterian had some of the best preachers, scholarly Scotch ministers who wrote brilliant sermons. With its Tiffany windows and majestic sanctuary, First Presbyterian was—and still is—a beautiful building, and I loved it from the very moment I walked in the front door. A great church such as this is often a miraculous group effort. There is more to it than physical beauty. When I sit in First Presbyterian today, I can't help but marvel at the fierce commitment that brings a building like this to life. I think of hundreds of people who labored behind the scenes, laying bricks, erecting walls, raising money, making the countless decisions that are required for such a project. For some perhaps it was just a job to be done, but one senses a collective spirit in their work that suffuses the building with a special beauty.

After my mother, brother, and I joined my father in Philadelphia, we all became regulars at First Presbyterian. Every Sunday we would leave our apartment in Germantown and drive the winding road along the Wissahickon Creek to downtown Philadelphia. On the way home, we always discussed the sermons or church business.

When I was thirty, I became a church deacon, a new position for a woman to assume in those days. Later I was nominated to become the first woman on the session, the church's governing lay body. Though the Presbyterian Church had allowed women to become church elders since 1930, many individual churches did not accept the idea. In those churches women were confined to dusting the sanctuary and raising funds.

The pastor of First Presbyterian was among those who felt the business of the church was a man's job. On the day my name was put forth, he stood before the group assembled to hear the nominations and, in a booming voice, said, "No! As long as I am pastor of this church there will be no woman on the session." I felt as if I had been slapped in the face. At first I was mortified—and then furious. The incident built up in me a well of resentment against the church's backwardness. My father, who was on the session himself, was shocked that I would not be allowed to follow in his footsteps as a church elder.

Though there have been countless exemplary church leaders, I have long felt that church practices sometimes produce dictators. Benevolent despots have been canonized by life membership on the session. Aggressive people who could manipulate, even bulldoze, others into compliance, have been rewarded with long tenures and unchallenged domination of the Sunday church schools, administrative committees, and adult associations.

In an active church you may find, in microcosm, the same sort of political maneuverings and petty disputes that exist in city hall and on Capitol Hill. Upon discovering this, many people are appalled and disillusioned. They expect church life and its relationships to be as ethereal as the stained glass windows and the music. But you must expect as much human failing inside a church as in any other institution.

I have always liked the intellectual quality of Presbyterianism, its constant analysis of ethical values and social justice. Though Presbyterians are often thought of as stodgy and close-minded, there is a thread of passionate soul-searching that runs through our history. Presbyterians love to argue. The Church's history in this country is a long series of debates over doctrinal correctness and the relationship of the church to the world.

The Presbyterian Church has a representative form of government whose structure is similar to that of the U.S. government. The General Assembly, the

church's governing body, which comprises representatives from around the country, meets once a year,
and its sessions are often as heated and contentious as
a meeting of the House of Representatives. The Assembly promotes participation and democratic decision-making in the Church. It adopts a national budget
every year and issues decrees on everything from litur-
gical changes to the Church's stand on world affairs,
overseeing the Church in the way the federal government oversees the states and municipalities. The Assembly comprises representatives from the Church's
38 synods and 257 presbyteries, collective bodies that
represent regional groupings of churches. Thus, it
represents a great diversity of opinion and experience.

I remember how proud my father was in 1924 to
sign the *Auburn Affirmation*, a document written by
theologians that challenged the doctrinal fanaticism of
church conservatives. My father was conservative
politically but liberal theologically. He rejected strict
adherence to every syllable of the Bible and would
have been shocked and enraged by the success of fun-
damentalists like Billy Graham and Jimmy Bakker.

Yet he loved theological skirmishes and thrived on
them intellectually. My father, as well as my courses in
biblical literature at college and at Union Theological
Seminary, encouraged me to think deeply about my
faith and to take it on my own terms. I came to view
much of the Bible as allegory, as a story with profound
meaning for our world today. I don't accept the Presbyterian interpretation of the Christian faith in every
particular, but I'm deeply rooted in my faith nonethe-

less. Most importantly, I believe there is a spirit within us all—the Holy Spirit is a good name for it—that sustains us when we are knocked down.

The Old Testament and its recurring themes of mercy and justice—which are particularly relevant to our world today—have had an ongoing influence on me. I remember those stories of the Christian saints that I learned as a child. Those saints had such persistence—they didn't know what it meant to give up. "Stick up for what you believe in!"—that's what their lives said to me.

Christianity holds that people are fallible and yet capable of great good. I believe there is an ultimate judgment by God of what we have done as a community, a nation, and as human beings. "What does the Lord require of you but to do justice, to love kindness and to walk humbly with your God?" (Micah 6:8) I like to think I brought these words to bear on my work as a social activist.

In 1948, after the YWCA's USO division was phased out, I landed a job as a program coordinator for the General Alliance for Unitarian and Other Liberal Christian Women, in Boston. Once again I was working with a group of women with a broad social outlook. I felt right at home. My father was fond of joking with his Presbyterian friends that I was doing missionary work among the Unitarians.

I liked Boston. My office was on the third floor of the Unitarian national headquarters at 25 Beacon Street. From one window I had a view of Boston Common and from the other, of the magnificent statehouse. For the first few months, I lived in Cambridge, in the home of the director of public relations of Harvard University. He and his wife were delightful friends. I loved to walk through Harvard Square, which wasn't as hectic then as it is today. Eventually, I moved to an apartment on Charles Street, overlooking the river. It was within walking distance to work.

I had a brief romance with Walt, a divorced man who was head of maintenance in my office building. Walt was black, and because we knew we would attract attention, we couldn't go to restaurants together and instead would spend evenings in my apartment. We would sometimes walk along the river at night or spend a day at the beach. Though interracial romances were unconventional in those days, I didn't think twice about it. It was a short-lived affair that ended when I left Boston after two years.

Worried about my parents' increasing frailty, I had become anxious to return to Philadelphia. My mother had developed severe arthritis and was confined to a wheelchair. My father was too frail to manage even with the help of a part-time nurse. My parents needed me and wanted me at home. At that time part of the national headquarters of the Presbyterian Church of the USA was located in Philadelphia. My father discovered that there was an opening as assistant secretary of the church's Social Education and Action Department. It was an executive position and was just the kind of job I was looking for. The interview went well and I was offered the job. I took it gladly.

The Social Education and Action Department was the church's social conscience. It was responsible for analyzing public issues and lobbying on the Church's behalf. During the '50s and '60s, when I worked for the department, many Presbyterians, and Christians everywhere, were coming to believe that the churches must worry not just about individual morality, but about right and wrong in public affairs. It wasn't enough to just proclaim the Word, we had to go out and do it.

From the start, the department was controversial within the Church itself. When it was established in 1936, an editorial in *The Presbyterian*, a newspaper published by one Presbyterian faction, complained that the new department "sounds too communistic, or too fascistic or what you please, rather than Calvinistic or Christian."

The social action department came out of the same tradition of Christian social reform that gave birth to the YWCA, the temperance movement, the Society for the Prevention of Cruelty to Children, and the Salvation Army. These great movements, inspired by the evangelical revival of the late nineteenth century, demanded that Christians take on more of the problems of real human beings. Out of deep religious conviction, they wrestled with the complexities of twentieth-century life. Their influence can be seen in hundreds of organizations and government social programs today.

At the YWCA I had worked to bring better working conditions, education, and enrichment to working-class women. In the social action department, my co-workers and I urged churchgoers to take progressive stands on important social issues: desegregation, urban housing, McCarthyism, the Cold War, nuclear arms. We believed that without powerful institutions like the Presbyterian Church advocating reform, many problems would go unsolved.

Every year, the Church's presbyteries and synods individually considered what stand they wanted the Church as a whole to take on important social issues. They would submit their proposals to us and we, in turn, would present them to the Assembly. Our work brought the tensions between liberals and conservatives in the Church to the fore, and our proposals frequently caused fiery debate on the floor of the Assembly. Department members, sometimes called commies and kooks by conservatives, tended to be more liberal than the Church membership at large. Whenever I was making a speech before a group that I suspected might be a little cool on my ideas, I would dress in an especially becoming, though prim, hat. You know, they say the Indians hunted Buffalo with Buffalo skins on their heads.

Though we were the target of attacks by people like J. Howard Pew, the Sun Oil founder and chairman who vehemently believed the Church should not take stands on secular issues, we were often successful in getting the Assembly to adopt our proposals. During the '50s and '60s, the Church came to be known for its enlightened stances on many issues, particularly civil rights.

Back then the Presbyterian Church of the USA had most of its national offices in the Witherspoon Building—off Broad Street in the center of the city, a few blocks from City Hall and the all-male Union League, where the city's most influential businessmen gathered for lunch. It seemed a fitting location for the bureaucracy of a Church that had supplied this country with a wealth of bankers and businessmen.

The Witherspoon Building, named after John Witherspoon, a Presbyterian who was the only clergyman to sign the Declaration of Independence, was a monolithic nineteenth-century building with nine-foot statues of the Church's founding fathers ornamenting its facade. There were once dozens of stone "Lions of Judah" designed by the famous sculptor Alexander Calder across the top of the building. They began to crumble forty years ago and little bits of stone would rain down on pedestrians.

When workmen came to remove the lions with a jackhammer, Ben Sissel, a minister who worked in our department, scrambled up to the roof to rescue them. He persuaded the workmen to give the figures to him. Ben became known as the guy with the lion concession, although he never actually sold them. He gave one to me and I still have it in my basement.

Until it was dwarfed by skyscrapers, the Witherspoon Building was so solid and serious and purposeful; as decreed by the General Assembly, it was "an ornament to the city, a fit exponent of the strength and capacity of the Presbyterian Church and a center of Beneficent power and religious influence for the elevation and enlightenment of the whole country." Even so, shrewd, ruthless church politics went on within those walls.

I was slightly intimidated by it all at first—in a way I had never felt at the YWCA. There were very few women in executive positions like the one I held. The Church hired women as secretaries and, for some reason, to operate the elevators that stood at the end of the building's massive marble lobby. Women would work the huge levers that opened and closed the elevator doors. Their visible station in the elevators seemed symbolic to me of the limitations on a woman's mobility within the church hierarchy. People used to joke that when the doors became automatic, the job would be so easy they would hire only men.

From the Witherspoon Building, Presbyterian literature was disseminated throughout the country—a massive effort. In 1948 the Church had begun an extremely ambitious Christian education program, the Faith and Life curriculum. The Church's Board of Christian Education published graded lessons, illustrated books, and magazines that helped spur the unprecedented growth of the Church during the 1950s. *Presbyterian Life*, also produced at the Witherspoon Building, was one of the most widely circulated religious journals in the country, and the Westminster Press, the Church's official publishing house, produced study editions of the Bible and books on Presbyterian history and studies.

One of my old friends from the USO, Mildred Kemm, was hired by the Church as a "curriculum gypsy." She sold the curriculum to churches and schools around the country, traveling almost ten months a year in a Studebaker that she called her "rolling apartment." Part of my duties included training clergy and laity in social justice issues and lobbying for positions taken by the General Assembly; thus my work also took me around the country. Traveling to churches and Presbyterian colleges, I felt like one of those early frontier ministers who "itinerated" from place to place, always without a congregation of his own.

The Presbyterian Church of the USA was one of the major Protestant denominations at the time. When I arrived at the Witherspoon Building in 1950, the Church was entering a period of explosive growth—as were many of the large Protestant denominations in the country. The war was over. The country was prospering and young couples were flocking to the suburbs and having large families. Church membership became as much a part of this new suburban culture as station wagons, shopping malls, and trim lawns. Pews were packed every Sunday. Thousands of young men were seeking entry into crowded seminaries.

Was the growth the sign of a spiritual awakening in the country? Would it last? Many of us thought not. In 1950 the National Council of Churches began a series of studies about the part religion plays in the decisions Americans must make about their daily work. A summary of the study's findings, *Ethics in a Business Society*, was written and reprinted in a popular thirty-five-cent edition. The Council had found that many Americans had only shallow ties to their churches. "It was not that they were irreligious," said the authors of *Ethics*. "Many of them were church-goers. It was simply that their religious experience did not seem to be relevant to the problems confronting them in earning their living. One gathered from their remarks that religion is something to one side, a social experience that is sometimes consoling and pleasant but one that does not strike very deep."

For many Presbyterians, the Church seemed to have no light to shed on the problems of buying and selling, earning a living, and getting along in this kind of world. At the same time, millions of people honestly concerned about such issues as racial justice, women's rights, and nuclear arms had written off the Church. The Social Education and Action Department was trying to bridge the gulf between the churches and real life, and to bring the tradition of prophetic protest and responsibility to modern churches that had become timid and conformist.

There were usually four of us working on the social education staff, all comrades in arms. I think we were the only department in the Witherspoon Building where everyone called each other by their first names. The department was headed by Rev. Clifford Earle, an eloquent, serious man who was trained at Princeton University and McCormick Theological Seminary. He spoke passionately about the need for laity and clergy to take an interest in social reform.

As we edited and wrote articles for *Social Progress*,

known as "the oldest journal of social comment in Presbyterianism," we came to know a great deal about public policy and social issues. I found it absorbing, an education in dozens of issues I had never studied before. I was always reading up on the latest figures on housing or employment or crime, and these would all factor into articles I wrote for *Social Progress* or proposals we brought to the yearly Assembly meetings. I liked to think of myself as bringing the social sciences to the Church. I remember once someone from another department in the Witherspoon Building came to our office in need of information on a particular issue. She asked for Dr. Earle and was told he was not in. She then asked for Ben Sissel, my great friend and co-worker, and was told that he too was out.

"But Margaret Kuhn is here," our eager secretary volunteered.

"No thanks," said the visitor. "I didn't want to know *that* much about it."

The social action office was on the eighth floor, three floors above the office of Eugene Carson Blake, the stated clerk of the General Assembly. During his tenure from 1951 to 1966, Blake elevated the position of stated clerk to denominational spokesman and spiritual leader. He was jokingly referred to as the Presbyterian pope.

Blake's office was guarded by his secretary, Mabel Hunt, who protected her boss with legendary zeal. However, I got to know the man behind the doors, and those of us in social action generally considered him to be our ally. A former quarterback at Princeton

University, Blake resembled the all-American football hero: hazel eyes, broad shoulders, square jaw. The Church had more prestige on Capitol Hill than it enjoys today, and Blake and other religious leaders were constantly sending communiqués to congressional leaders urging their support for various causes. At the time, our denomination had an office in a building across from the Supreme Court.

"Ministers must risk being wrong rather than be silent and safe," argued Blake, who spoke out against McCarthyism, segregation, anti-Catholic sentiments during Kennedy's campaign for president, and the Vietnam War. In 1963 he was arrested when he took part in efforts to desegregate a Baltimore amusement park. "Churchgoers should stop regarding God as a white, American idol," he remarked.

Though Blake understood the tension between liberals and conservatives and could be a skilled diplomat between the two camps, his action in Baltimore lost him the support of some conservatives. During his tenure the Church took some courageous stands and made many pronouncements on racial justice. In 1946 the General Assembly called for a "non-segregated church in a non-segregated society," and in 1956 it called upon Presbyterians to join in covenants of open occupancy to break down residential segregation. Our social action department took part in the organized fight for civil rights legislation, better housing in the cities, and government anti-poverty programs. There were many victories, and I look back on that era as testimony to the irrepressible power of the grass roots. When I think of the thousands of people who took to the streets to march in those years, I know that ordinary people can do extraordinary things.

Shortly after I started working in Philadelphia in 1950, I met a minister who occupied an executive position in the church. He was an extremely erudite man and as passionate about his work as I was about mine. About six feet tall, he wore glasses and was balding, not what most people would call physically attractive. Although he was married and had one teenage child, we were instantly drawn to each other and, not long after we met, began a fifteen-year love affair.

Our affair was illicit and highly secretive. Exposure would have ruined our careers and his marriage. To this day, I only mention his name to my dearest friends. Ever since I contemplated taking that train out of Cleveland with Paul Foulkes, the son of the minister at Old Stone, secrecy has been a habit in my love life. Early on, I took to separating my love affairs from the rest of my life.

There has always been more than just sexual attraction in my affairs. The minister was passionately interested in international issues and the Church's social causes. We talked constantly about our work and our views. Ours was an affair of the mind as well as of the heart.

We frequently traveled together on Church business and would spend time alone with each other on these occasions. He would come to my hotel room or I would go to his. When he was out of town without me, he would send me postcards—from foreign countries he would always write in the language of the place he was visiting. He would also send me blue crystal paperweights. He visited me at home occasionally. My parents knew him well and, in fact, his family and my family often celebrated Thanksgiving and Christmas together. No one—except my mother, who sensed our involvement without my telling her—knew of our relationship.

The issue of fidelity is a complicated one. Many women who become involved with married men sicken themselves with guilt. I did not. I considered his marriage to be his affair. I was troubled occasionally by the thought of his wife, but probably not enough.

There are so many rules and regulations that govern our lives—even today, in an era of relative sexual freedom. But there are certain natural urges and strong attractions that overpower the rules. Sometimes you act on these urges and sometimes you don't.

I remember the strong prohibition against masturbation in my childhood. Whenever I touched myself my mother would react with such shock—it was like an electric prod. Even so, at night when I was alone and investigated my own body in the dark, I never felt shame. I felt I was doing something right and good.

Sex was still taboo for single women in the 1950s, but I didn't let this stop me. A popular book of the day was *A Woman Doctor Looks at Love and Life*, in which Dr. Marian Hilliard offered advice to America's unmarried women: "Read a detective story. Visit a friend with five children under ten. Take a very hot bath and plan your next year's vacation. Avoid listening to jazz records; the tom-tom beat is bad for you. Join a badminton club where unescorted women do not feel out of place."

There is hope, she told them. "By the age of 40–45 desires diminish and die down. The best is yet to be when jazz no longer disturbs and arouses!" Those poor souls.

My relationship with my married friend was especially tender. I knew it was right. It was the first time I felt the intimacy that can come from a longtime affair.

By that time I had had two mastectomies. The first occurred when I was thirty-six and working at the YWCA. I had a lump in my breast and went to a Germantown surgeon, a doctor who was considered one of the best in the area. I was intimidated by his reputation and did not question his plans for the procedure. I will always remember the incident as a revelation; I found out just how cold and inhuman a doctor could be. He truly botched the job. The lump turned out to be a bloody cyst and my breast could have been saved, but he removed it. I contracted a bad infection. When I went to the doctor's office for postoperative treatment, I fainted as I walked into the examining room. When I came to, the doctor was looking down at me disdainfully. "So, I see we have a fainty woman on our hands," he said to the nurse.

I had a second mastectomy five years later. The second lump had been diagnosed as cancerous. This time I found a better doctor and the experience was a much happier affair. Though I was completely flat-chested by the age of forty, I was not devastated by the change. I bought some cotton padding and forgot about the whole thing, convinced that I was not interested in the type of man who would be bothered by it. I took no less pleasure in my appearance. I always enjoyed dressing in nice clothes and took pains over my wardrobe. I remember sitting on a train or plane and sewing little frills and flourishes on the hats I would wear on a business trip.

My first love has always been to work with groups. In the summers we had training schools in which we taught Presbyterians how to lobby, how to develop working papers, and how to conduct seminars in their own communities about social responsibility. We would go into a community and help the church members identify the powerful people and organizations in their city or town so that when the church took on a community project they would know whom to approach for support. It was our contention that every church should engage in a continuing analysis of the community it serves. Just as a chamber of commerce emphasizes the good qualities of a community, a church should look to the core of its problems.

In some conservative communities, especially in the South, our ideas were branded as socialist. In 1954

I wrote a pamphlet titled "The Christian Woman and Her Household": it preached "responsible consumership," urging women to engage in "friendly protest against anything we consider wrong," to refuse to buy products produced under unfair labor conditions, to study local housing conditions, and to investigate the Church's own labor and economic practices, its investments and real estate holdings. Many of these ideas were similar to those I had written about for the YWCA.

The pamphlet was burned in protest by a meeting of a chapter of the Presbyterian Women's Organization in Lexington, Kentucky. In Lexington I was labeled a Communist. Perhaps, in spirit, I was.

I would sometimes run into the same sort of trouble at the General Assembly. The social action staff and our standing committee would haggle over that year's social pronouncements before deciding whether to present them to the entire Assembly. Standing committee members were elected by the Assembly members, some of whom were very keen to put conservatives on the committee. We kept the committee members on their toes, asking them to act on the most controversial issues of the day. It was not unusual for a committee meeting to last for many hours and become quite lively, with people yelling and pounding their fists.

I remember one particularly fierce debate over the early proposals for Medicare. In the late '50s, as the battle over proposals for a national health program were heating up in Congress, I did a little study—a very amateurish one—in which I looked at health care in this country. I was appalled when I read the figures on the cost of major illnesses. I arranged a Presbyterian conference on health care at the Palmer House, a big hotel on the Loop in Chicago. The president of the American Medical Association, the leading opponent of all proposals for a national health insurance, and Nelson Cruikshank, a Methodist minister who was an executive for the AFL-CIO and was leading the fight for what would later become Medicare, were among those who spoke at the conference, which was heated from the beginning. I'll never forget the venom in that meeting room.

In 1960, as a result of that meeting and my research, I brought a very modest report to the General Assembly that urged the Church to study seriously the current proposals for a federal health insurance program. I hoped that once a study was conducted, the Church would decide to support the Medicare proposals. The report was leaked to the AMA. Every one of the Assembly commissioners that year—all nine hundred of them—got at least half a dozen telegrams delivered to their seats on the floor of the Assembly. The telegrams were from doctors urging them not to vote in favor of my report.

There were four doctors among the commissioners and they, of course, vehemently opposed changes in the medical system. They were fond of calling it "socialized medicine," playing on popular fears of socialism.

I was astounded that my relatively harmless request had generated such a storm. We had a terrific battle in the Social Education and Action standing committee, which had to either approve or reject my recommendation. About sixteen of us sat in a tiny, overcrowded room for fifteen hours, leaving only to go to the bathroom. I trembled as I discussed my proposal. The chairman was Ed Stinson, of Omaha, a huge fellow—about six and a half feet tall with size sixteen shoes and a voice like a steam engine. He bellowed all day against my report. An eloquent layman from Indianapolis argued in favor of the proposed study and saved the day. The study was authorized. But, to my disappointment, it came to no effect. The Church did not take a stand either for or against a new federal health program. Five years later Medicare was established. As it turned out, it was not as bad for the AMA's members as feared. Doctors everywhere have cashed in on a program that they have exploited and almost destroyed.

In addition to health care, housing was one of my prime interests in the '60s. The previous decade had been a time of explosive suburban growth and inner city decay. From 1935 to 1950, nine million new homes were constructed in our country; less than 1 percent were available to nonwhite citizens. In every American city, there were desperate slums. I remember inviting Richardson Dilworth, then the mayor of Philadelphia, to speak before a group of Presbyterians and city planners in the board room of the Witherspoon Building. The mayor spoke movingly of the suburbs as the "white noose strangling the city."

Today, as Philadelphia grapples with financial insolvency, brought on in part by the flight of whites from the city, his words seem prescient.

Back then, a few large cities had well-functioning citizens' committees on housing. Many more were needed. We felt churches could and must play a decisive role in bringing together representatives from civic organizations and government to try to influence housing policies and to initiate more long-range planning. Every year for ten years, starting in the early '60s, I arranged a housing conference concurrent with the annual convention of the American Institute of Planners. We would meet in the same city as the planners, inviting them to attend our meetings and grappling with the same issues. We raised questions about their objectives and tried to have input on urban policy.

However, the Church's Board of National Missions fought us at every turn. The board was the largest and oldest of the Church's governing boards and carried on mission work in each U.S. state, Cuba, the Dominican Republic, and Puerto Rico. It had educational, medical, and evangelistic programs among black, Hispanic, and Asian communities in this country. Representatives from the board would also attend AIP conventions—for wholly different reasons than we did. They wanted most of all to be sure that the cities set aside prime sites for new church development. The board didn't give a hoot about urban renewal or housing policies. They just wanted to be sure the Church got the best spots. The Church sought its own best interests at the expense of the city.

In the late '60s, I also worked as one of several Presbyterian observers for the Church at the United Nations. There was an uneasy alliance between the social action staff and the foreign missionaries, whose ventures we would not always support. The missionaries were committed to the Arabs and those of us in social action were committed to the Jews. We had some really knock-down drag-out arguments.

I remember how we tried to bring Arab and Israeli representatives to seminars to discuss the problems in the Middle East. It was a perilous thing to set up because neither the Arabs nor the Israelis would respond in the presence of the other. They wouldn't even come into a room by way of the same entrance for fear of bumping into one another.

The Church was often in a state of flux. In the late '60s and early '70s, there were several reorganizations and our denomination merged with smaller denominations to become the United Presbyterian Church in the USA. With the mergers, staffing of the social action department was changed and cut back. Clifford Earle went to the Interchurch Center in New York. Some wondered whether I might head the social action office. I was never asked to take the job, and did not want the position. I was always good at thinking up ideas and developing programs, but administration was not my cup of tea. Instead, I was transferred to New York, to work on a program called Renewal and Extension of the Ministries.

Many people, women in particular, lost jobs or promotions because of the mergers and restructurings. Women continued to work as secretaries for the Church, but still, not many made it to executive positions like the one I had. My salary was about four thousand dollars less than it would have been for a man. When I broached the subject with my superiors, they would say, "Well, it's regrettable."

I began—very quietly—talking to other women about the situation. A group of us met whenever we could for lunch. We really bared our souls to each other, sharing long-repressed feelings about our inferior status. We decided to form a group working openly for equality for women in the Church. Our real coup was getting the General Assembly to approve a three-year commission on the status of women.

While there were few women ministers and few women on the various boards, agencies, councils, and judicatories of the Church, they were a significant majority of the Church's membership. The 1969 "Report of the Special Commission on the Status of Women in Society and in the Church," the three-year study we had proposed, condemned the unequal status of women in the church. It described the average church woman:

> She's prepared tons of food and washed thousands of dishes for church suppers. She's taught hundreds of children in the primary department of the church school. She's outfitted countless babies in missionary layettes. She's

always available to lead devotionals in circle, guild or association. She has denominational documents on everything from Amos to Zanzibar, piled three feet high in her basement. She's helped redecorate the manse and the church house whenever the trustees and minister have decided the time has come. . . . But, no nominating committee has ever asked her to be a deacon or a trustee or an elder, and it has not occurred to her that they should.

That first commission did not succeed in bringing about change, but a second commission recommended a new department that gave women a power base within the national structure of the Church.

Though the Church had begun to lose membership by the mid-'60s, I think it had become in some ways a better Church. It had been through a period of intense self-examination and emerged whole.

In 1964, just after Lyndon Johnson's War on Poverty was declared, I took a six-month sabbatical to teach a course on ethics and poverty at San Francisco Seminary, in Marin County, one of the country's most affluent areas. It's a beautiful campus, set on a hill. On a clear day, you can see San Francisco Bay. I'll never forget the enthusiasm of those seminarians, who were influenced by the student protests in Berkeley. We had so much to discuss: What is justice? What is good work that satisfies people? Is capitalism the best system? They were the sort of questions that ten years before would have been considered inappropriate for a seminary classroom. I remember that one of the students had put himself through college driving a truck and had joined the Teamsters, which he called "the best Goddamn union in the country." For seminarians to say something like this ten years before would have been unthinkable.

In the past seminarians had largely confined their fieldwork to churches. I sent them out into the community and told them that none of them would pass unless they found some evidence of poverty in Marin County. They found Hunter's Point, a poor black community in a sea of white affluence.

Today, as the Church preoccupies itself with survival in an age of growing fundamentalism, much of the social dimension of the Gospel has been lost. It distresses me not that the congregations of great churches have become small, but that people continue to use the Church as a refuge from the world's problems. So much of the emphasis today is on escape from stress. Some American ministers achieve a great hearing by using self-help slogans to lull people into a dangerous tranquility. There's too much talk about "burn-out."

I'd rather see a healthy discontent. Books on peace of mind may be best-sellers, but the American public needs a lot of disturbing. Instead of avoiding all the world's problems or being overcome by them, I like to see them as an invitation.

CHAPTER 6

A Graceful Exit

When I was a child, death was an event that took place in one of my grandmother's bedrooms. I always admired the women in my grandmother's house who would band together to nurse a sick relative. It was draining, backbreaking work.

When the sick failed to recover, a funeral would take place in the big house on Eagle Street. My grandmother died when I was six years old, and her body was laid out in the front parlor. For the first time, I wasn't permitted to enter the room. "No! No! Don't go in there," I remember my aunts saying in a stern, hushed voice. I felt slighted—as if I had been left out of some great excitement.

A few years later, a friend of the family died and I got my first opportunity to go to a funeral. I remember how excited I was before the big event—it was a rite of passage, a chance to act like an adult. But my initial glimpse of the corpse, its ashen face resembling no person I had ever known, unraveled me. I didn't sleep for many, many nights. To a young child, death seems so unnatural. I couldn't imagine then that over time it would lose its power to shock.

My father died in 1955 in our apartment in Germantown after a relatively happy old age. After the Bradstreet company merged with R. G. Dun and Co., my father was replaced as district manager by a younger man who respected and admired him. He kept my father on part-time as a troubleshooter handling difficult contracts. Thus, my father was never idle as he grew old. He read constantly; I remember him always bent over a book or newspaper with our cat, Toby, sitting by his side.

We were reconciled in those years. I was fifty years old and no longer angry about his interference in my love life. My father accepted our different political views and felt pride for my work. He was not easy to love, but I loved him. He had given me backbone and perseverance.

When he was eighty-six, he started to fail rapidly. It was painful to see a man who took so much pride in his self-possession deteriorate. His heart was weak, forcing him to remain in bed and, for the first time in his life, rely totally on others. Our roles were reversed, and now I was making the decisions. A nurse became a fixture of our household and took care of him during his last frail months. Fortunately, the end came quickly. Within a few months after he fell ill, he died peacefully one morning with my mother and me at his side.

I mourned and missed him, feeling as any loving daughter would on her father's death. But I also felt liberated, like a woman whose marriage to a demanding and controlling husband has come to an end.

Eager to secure my future financially and to start a new life, I immediately began to hunt for a house after his death. My father, never forgetting his own poor investments, had warned me repeatedly against buying real estate. He was extremely conservative with money—indeed, he had to be for he had lost a great deal during the Depression. For years, my own instincts had told me to buy a house of my own, but I held back so as not to offend him. Also, it was unusual for a single woman to buy her own house. Why would a woman *need* a home of her own? We were expected to stay with our parents, living an extended childhood. Low wages also made it difficult, if not impossible, for most women to purchase property.

I knew I wanted to stay in Germantown. It was my home in the way no other place had been. I loved its old cobblestone streets and stately Victorian stone houses, its Revolutionary battle sites and teeming shopping district. While other sections of the city had become exclusively black or white, poor or middle-class, Germantown, which had been colonized by German settlers in the 1600s, was mixed. There was a great feeling of history and flux.

By the late 1950s, Germantown was no longer a booming industrial community and its fashionable neighborhoods were declining. There was increasing racial tension. I recall many of my white friends and acquaintances talking about moving out because *they* were moving in. I *preferred* to live in an integrated community, not simply because segregation was against my principles. There is a vitality to integrated neighborhoods that you can't find in homogenized suburbs.

In 1957 I found the perfect house—a Victorian twin a few blocks from the Germantown apartments where my mother, brother, and I lived. The house was made of a glistening micaceous stone dug from a quarry that ran through parts of Germantown. It reminded me of my grandmother's house. There was a back porch, a garden, a front porch and an elegant carved banister along the front stairway—more than I had ever dreamed of owning myself. I could see my grandmother bustling about, effortlessly presiding over family dinners for twenty.

The house was selling for $12,600, an attractive price at the time. I put a small down payment on it to hold the sale and began to shop around for a mortgage. To my shock and dismay, I discovered that it was almost impossible for a single woman to secure a mortgage from a bank. We were considered "undesirable risks," even if we had saved enough for a down payment. An unmarried woman, it was believed, might at any time leave or lose her job. The Presbyterian Church gave mortgages to ministers and men in executive positions like the one I held, but did not give them to women.

Nevertheless, I was determined to get my house and decided to wait for the right opportunity to appear. On New Year's Eve that year, my family held a party in our apartment. One of our guests was a member of the board of the Presbyterian Home for Widows and Single Women. I mentioned my difficulties.

"I can get you a mortgage," he said. "I'm sure the Home would be willing to give it to you." I was grateful for his offer and cautiously optimistic. I went to the Home for an interview and to fill out forms. A few months later, I was granted a mortgage with a 5.5 percent interest rate. I guess the Home saw it as an act of preventive charity. I was thrilled.

I moved into the house with my mother and brother in 1958. My mother, who by that time was ninety, had supported wholeheartedly my decision to buy a house and loved the place. I remember her sitting on the porch—we hadn't had a porch since our Cleveland days—and watching the passing scene. She liked to sit out there in her wheelchair, all bundled up against the cold, waving to people on the street.

My mother still brightened up a room just by her presence, and I loved coming home to her. She was a member of the Mount Airy Literary Club and carried a small satchel in which she stashed clippings and jokes to share at the club meetings. She was fond of making up humorous words. She would say someone was "solemncholy" or had gotten into a "pucker-snatch," an unresolved difficulty.

She was very infirm and had crippling arthritis. Her hands were stiff and gnarled—just like mine are today—and she could not feed herself. We would feed her and she would open her mouth like a little bird—I will never forget it. One day I sat with my arm around her on the sofa in our new living room. It seemed as we sat there that she got smaller and smaller, as if she were fading. She looked up at me and said, "You

know, sometimes I don't feel like a person anymore."
The remark shook me deeply. My mother had never
expressed such hopelessness.

I held her closer in my arms. "You are more
human than ever before," I said. "Look at how well
you've done despite your infirmities." Later I wept.

One day, about nine months after we had moved,
she fell out of bed and hit her head against the radia-
tor. She had an ugly bruise over her eye. I was with her
when she died two days later in the bedroom we had
made for her downstairs. I was holding her hand because she was restless and wakeful. She rolled over,
glanced at me and said, "I'm so tired." Resting her
head on my arm, she died. My sadness was immense.
We had understood, admired, and loved each other.

Her death affected my brother, Sam, profoundly.
Unfortunately, Sam was living at home again. Norristown State Hospital, like other mental institutions in
the '50s, was forced to make severe cuts because of a
loss of funds and the growing belief that the mentally
ill did not need to be confined to such places. Despite
our objections, Sam was deemed well enough to leave.
I didn't want him to come home, believing it would
make him regress and undo all the good that had been
done at Norristown. We arranged to have Sam live
nearby in a boarding home in Mount Airy, hoping
that he might be able to sustain some independence.
However, he demanded to come home, saying he
wanted to be near my mother. He returned shortly
before my father's death and never left again.

He clung to my mother, who always dealt with him

gently and with great affection. She denied the seriousness of his condition and babied him even when he was a man in his fifties. To my mother, the world "misunderstood" Sam.

After she was gone, he became more prone to violent fits of temper and infantile behavior. Sam did not like our new house. As before, he didn't adapt well to change. He sulked and brooded much of the time. He was extremely lonely, and there seemed little I could do to make his life better, short of staying with him all the time. He could occasionally be distracted from his depression. There was a Ping-Pong table in the basement, and he would have kids from the neighborhood come in and play with him. He was a strange companion to them. My brother had a very sweet, loving side to him that surfaced when he played with children and teenagers. His only other companion was our Persian cat, Toby, whom he adored. They spent every moment together during the day and slept together at night. I will never forget the sight of Sam, who by then weighed nearly three hundred pounds, lying in bed next to that small cat.

Sam resented my involvement in my work and that I traveled frequently. "Why don't you stay home and take care of me?" he demanded. He had a horrible fear of flying and would tell me that I would die if I traveled by plane. He couldn't comprehend that I could be here one day and halfway across the country the next. Reassuring him that I would be back, I would leave.

The Church had reorganized its operations and

moved some of its national offices to New York. I was transferred to New York in 1965, but kept my home in Philadelphia to be close to my brother. By then, my fifteen-year love affair was all but over. Over the course of the previous few years, my friend and I had drifted apart. He was unhappy with the direction his career had taken and became embittered with life. He took to drinking and began to avoid me. I was puzzled and hurt.

The final break came with a quarrel, a bitter disagreement about the Vietnam War. He had expertise in international affairs, and I had always respected his opinions in this area. During the many years we worked together, we were in perfect agreement on most matters. But I strongly opposed United States involvement in Vietnam, believing it was immoral and illegal; to my shock, he supported it. It was so out of character. One day we had a heated argument over the issue and suddenly it was clear that our relationship was over.

Months later, when he was ill and in the hospital, I went to visit him, not quite sure about my motives. I didn't expect a full reconciliation, but I hoped some friendship between us could survive. My friend hardly spoke to me and abruptly dismissed me shortly after I arrived. "I think you'd better go now," he said. I complied.

Whatever sense of loss I felt I quickly buried in my work. Five days a week I commuted to New York, and on those mornings I would rise and be out the door before 7:15 A.M. Invariably, I found myself running—in bad weather, slipping and sliding—down the hill to the Upsal train station, with my coat unbuttoned and my hair not yet combed into a bun. I had an uncanny knack for arriving just as the train was pulling in. The Chestnut Hill West dropped me off in North Philadelphia. Amtrak's 8:10 train stopped there to pick up about twenty of us who made the pilgrimage to New York. Over time, we became friends and watched out for each other. We would congregate in one car and read, talk, doze off.

At Pennsylvania Station I rushed to the Seventh Avenue express subway, which took me to 96th Street, where I jumped on an uptown local to 116th Street. From there I walked the four blocks to the Interchurch Center at 120th Street, where most days I reached my office on the eighth floor promptly at 9:45.

In 1969 I was working as a program executive for the Church's Council on Church and Race, but was involved in a number of social action projects, including a subcommittee on the problems of the old. Since the 1961 White House Conference on Aging, which I attended as a Church observer, I had developed an interest in problems of the aged. My interest in these issues was not personal. The facts appealed to me as an activist. Many of us in the churches were concerned about the soaring poverty among the elderly and the staggering growth of the country's aged population. By 1969 there were 20 million people sixty-five years or older, and the number was growing at a rate of 900 a day. Nearly one-fourth of the aged population was living below the poverty line. Medical costs were sky-rocketing. Private pensions were unreliable and social services for the old were inadequate.

Dissatisfaction among the nation's old had been growing for two decades. When the Senate Subcommittee on the Problems of the Aged and Aging held hearings around the country in 1959, older Americans lined up to testify about the trials of their lives. They spoke of loneliness, destitution, and alienation.

The Church's interest in the old was largely confined to administering to the sick and dying and running retirement homes for well-to-do Presbyterians. Many Church officials, failing to see that the old needed vastly more than the Church was giving them, did not detect the rebellion brewing. I remember visiting John MacKay, the former president of Princeton Theological Seminary, at a Presbyterian retirement home in northern New Jersey. MacKay, whom I respected enormously, hated the place. "Maggie," he said, his face reddening with anger, "this is a glorified playpen."

The description seemed to apply to so many programs for "senior citizens"—a label I had come to loathe as another euphemism for the old. Such programs were almost exclusively recreational, things like bingo and arts and crafts. There seemed to be an apathy and malaise among the people in these programs that I could not attribute to old age itself. The women all wore polyester pantsuits with the same cut. There was a heart-wrenching monotony to their days. Was this what old age was meant to be?

In the late '60s I was elected to the board of four

rather posh Church retirement homes. The board's management style was autocratic. Meetings were dominated by two elderly lawyers. The residents' affairs committee comprised directors of the four institutions and representatives of the ladies' auxiliary. When I asked the chairman why no actual residents were on the committee, I was told that "the directors know what the residents need and want and are encouraged to bring these needs to the attention of the board." I was appalled at their total disregard for what the residents themselves had to say.

Not long after, a group of us formed a committee and proposed that the General Assembly recommend that all Church-related homes have a program council elected by the residents and resident participation on their boards. Though the idea was rejected, I brought the recommendation to the board of the retirement homes. One elderly board member sniffed derisively and said, "That would happen in this board over my dead body." The measures were not adopted. The incident taught me an important lesson: Many rich and powerful old people—particularly men who serve on prestigious boards of directors—have trouble identifying with their less fortunate peers. They wish it to appear that they themselves are not old.

Truthfully, in those years I didn't think of myself as about to enter the ranks of the nation's old either. I was just me—neither young, old, nor middle-aged. All of that changed when I was sixty-four. About seven months before my sixty-fifth birthday, the man who supervised the Council on Church and Race where I worked came to talk to me. To my utter shock, he asked if I would retire that summer.

I had never given retirement much thought. My sixty-fifth birthday was in August, but I had hoped the Church would ask me to stay on in my job on a year-to-year basis, as they had done with other executives of retirement age. As I felt energetic enough to go on for many years, the idea of retiring struck me as ludicrous and depressing. My work was my whole life. I couldn't envision myself with no serious purpose in life and cut off from the wide circle of friends at work. I was worried I'd end up becoming completely immersed in the care of my aging brother.

In the end I had no choice but to retire. In the following weeks the Board of Christian Education insisted I adhere to the Church's traditional retirement age. "We mean to be kind," I was told. "We know how hard it has been for you to commute and take care of your brother at the same time." What could I do? What could I say to change their minds? Nothing, I realized. I opted for a graceful exit.

We agreed I would stay until the end of the year, which would give me time to get my things in order and prepare for my new life. In the first month after I was ordered to retire, I felt dazed and suspended. I was hurt and then, as time passed, outraged. I could imagine how my Aunt Paulina must have felt when the railroad company denied her funeral expenses for her husband's burial. Something clicked in my mind and I saw that my problem was not mine alone. I came to feel a great kinship with my peers and to believe that something was fundamentally wrong with a system that had no use for people like us.

Instead of sinking into despair, I did what came most naturally to me: I telephoned some friends and called a meeting. Six of us, all professional women associated with nonprofit social and religious groups, met for lunch. We were all facing retirement. Eleanor French had been director of the student division of the World YWCA in Geneva, Helen Smith worked for the United Church of Christ, Polly Cuthbertson was director of the American Friends Service Committee College Program and had been involved in the YWCA Student Christian Movement, Anne Bennett was a religious educator and had worked on the Women's Strike for Peace, and Helen Baker was former editor of *The Churchwoman* and a reporter at the United Nations. All of us were veteran activists. All of us had energy to spare.

At that lunch we talked about the shock of retirement. We didn't *feel* old. In fact, we felt more radical and full of new ideas, more opinionated and less constrained by convention than we were when we graduated from college. We knew our lives had reached a sort of climax, not an ending. Yet we felt disturbed that we had few role models. Many of our mothers and grandmothers had been active up to the very end of their lives, but they were at home. We wanted to continue to be involved in social action bearing on the important public issues of the day—war and peace, the presidential elections, poverty, civil liberty. How should we go about it?

Being the good bureaucrats we were, we decided to call another meeting. Each of us knew other people who were in the same predicament and were anxious to work on something important. My office at work was next to a Xerox machine, so it was easy to slip over there and whip out copies of a notice for a meeting. We designated an evening in May for a gathering at the International House at Columbia University. The topic of the evening: "Older Persons and the Issues of the Seventies." Our notice about the event stated, "Older persons in our society constitute a great national resource which has largely been unrecognized, undervalued and unused. The purpose of our meeting is to consider how retirees can be involved in new and really significant ways. There should be no limit to our thinking and dreaming."

The meeting was a smashing success. About one hundred people came, including many who had heard about it second-hand. There was a palpable energy in the air. We agreed we should all band together to form a new social action organization. There was unanimous agreement that the issue we needed to address first was the Vietnam War, which we all staunchly opposed. All of us had lived through war and some of us had fought on the front or worked in armament plants. It wasn't just that we were all pacifists; we felt that our country's intervention in Southeast Asia was deeply misguided. We felt at one with the young war protesters and were disturbed that more of our generation were not speaking out. We organized a small money-raising effort to enable Anne Bennett to go to

Hanoi at Christmas with messages for American prisoners, and we began to attend anti-war rallies. We also
sent one of our group to Canada with care packages
for draft resisters.

In the following months we met in Philadelphia,
Princeton, Washington, and New York. We read everything from government reports to gerontological
studies to books about nursing homes. We thought
long and hard about other priorities for action. Some
members of the group wanted to work on the specific
problems of the aged, to become advocates for the old
by working on issues such as a national health plan,
pension rights, and age discrimination in the workplace. They also wanted to work to secure for older
persons the right and the opportunity to participate in
decision-making in the organizations that govern their
lives: the retirement homes, political parties, social
clubs, churches, and pension boards.

Others wanted to work primarily on larger public
issues, such as the war, housing, the 1972 presidential
elections, and health care. They felt the old, having the
benefit of life experience, the time to get things done,
and the least to lose by sticking their necks out, were
in a perfect position to serve as advocates for the
larger public good.

In a series of meetings that followed, we decided to
do it all. We would work for the old and we would
work for what we believed to be the common good.
We agreed upon a tentative name—the Consultation
of Older Persons—and set about planning our goals
and studying the issues. We were all eggheads and

knew how to get ahold of a problem and look at it inside and out.

The issue of the war in Vietnam put us in immediate contact with young people—the draft resisters and peace activists on college campuses. In 1971 we met at Foulkeways, a Quaker retirement community in suburban Philadelphia, with a number of students from universities and colleges in the region. Our guest speaker was Joseph Rhodes, then a Harvard graduate student and later a member of the Pennsylvania legislature. Joe, who served on Nixon's Presidential Commission on the Causes of Campus Unrest, discussed the commission's report, which had been completely ignored by the administration. We deliberated over the report and agreed to advocate for its recommendations. It was that meeting and Joe's enthusiasm about "age and youth in action" that convinced us that young people could play an important part in our organization.

In January 1971 Eleanor French died suddenly of a heart attack, and Helen Smith died of cancer a few weeks later. We all grieved. Any organization with old members suffers such losses. One of our member students, from Haverford College, said, "You old people are as transient as the students—here one year, gone the next." But our little movement pressed on. We would have to work around the high turnover in our membership.

Meanwhile, I had officially retired from my job. I remember my going-away party. My co-workers had gotten together and bought me a sewing machine—a beautiful gift, but a miscalculation of how I planned to spend my time. I never opened it. I set up a makeshift office at home and got to work. When it became clear that I was going to be as busy as ever, my brother grew more resentful. "You're my sister and you should take care of me," he scolded. "I don't want you to go out. It's your obligation to stay here with me."

I was troubled by his utter dependence on me and I knew neither of us would benefit if I gave up my life to see to his needs twenty-four hours a day. I invited two university students to live with us so that Sam would not be alone in the house. It was the wisest decision I ever made.

Early in 1971 I attended the Annual Conference on Aging at the University of Michigan's Institute of Gerontology. On my way to the conference in a hotel limousine, I met Hobart Jackson, a soft-spoken social worker who was director of the Stephen Smith Geriatric Center, a nursing home for poor blacks in Southwest Philadelphia. I had heard about how Jackson had transformed a dark, dank, and poorly managed retirement home into a model institution where residents participated on the board of directors. We instantly struck up a friendship.

Jackson and I were both hot on the issue of minority input at the upcoming Second White House Conference on Aging, scheduled to be held in Washington in the fall of 1971. The purpose of the conference was to develop a more comprehensive policy for older Americans and increased public awareness of older adults' needs and their potential as a national resource. We were concerned that, under Nixon, the event would be a political charade and would do little to create a new public image of the aged. With the heavy participation of gerontologists and social service professionals who were usually not themselves old, the emphasis seemed paternalistic.

There would be little participation of nonwhites in the conference and almost negligible data about the problems of elderly blacks and Hispanics. Yet recent studies had shown that the black aged, in particular, suffered a disproportionate share of the problems of the old. The Social Security system was based on white mortality tables and life expectancy. Many elderly blacks, especially men, did not live long enough to receive Social Security benefits. Furthermore, 50 percent of the black elderly population were poor, while 23 percent of elderly whites were poor. The majority of black elderly men in 1969 had annual incomes of less than $3,000. These startling facts were all but unknown to the Senate Special Committee on Aging, and were routinely neglected in reports by the Census Bureau and other federal research bodies.

Jackson decided to organize what he called a "Black House Conference on Aging" to draw attention to these inequities. I thought it was a brilliant idea—right up my alley—and joined in the planning. Two weeks before the White House conference, nine hundred people, mostly elderly blacks, assembled at the New York Avenue Presbyterian Church in Washington, D.C., for a two-day meeting. Some people slept in the church all night while others stayed in hotels or with friends. The deacons made coffee and sandwiches and looked after us. During the day we held intensive sessions about the problems of the black aged. Our discussions led to the formation of the National Caucus on the Black Aged, and Jackson served as its first chair. We knew all this would make the organizers of the White House Conference nervous and we were right. Arthur Flemming, Nixon's appointee to head the White House Conference, called to request a meeting with us.

Before we met with Flemming, seventy-five of us marched from the church to the White House gates with a list of ten demands for reducing disparities between the black and white aged in health care, housing, and income. We also called for an immediate end to the war. We all felt the war was a catastrophe and that, with so much of the federal budget devoted to it, resolution of these fundamental domestic problems would be impossible.

Most of us in the march were women over sixty-five. When we discovered the gates were locked, we petitioned the guard to take our message to the president. Just then a team of police on horses approached us. Fannie Jefferson, the leader of the march, stood her ground and refused to heed the order to move away from the gates. Suddenly we heard whistles and the horses began to charge into the crowd. Some marchers scattered and others of us clustered around the gate. I was knocked to the ground in the crush. Fannie was handcuffed and whisked into a police car.

No one was seriously injured, but the event made

a lasting impression on me. It showed me that being old was no protection, even from physical assault. Fannie was charged with disorderly conduct, but the case was dropped after pressure from officials of the White House conference. In the end, our event had been a success. We drew attention to our demands. Flemming, a compassionate man with an innate sense of justice, agreed to arrange for more minority representation at the White House event and to add our issues to the agenda.

I was not a delegate to the conference, but determined to attend, I secured press credentials for myself and two young people who had joined the Consultation. Every day we wrote press releases criticizing the proceeds of the conference and made hundreds of copies. We infiltrated the press room and slipped a copy of each release on every reporter's chair. Reporters sought us out for interviews and we got great coverage.

On the third day of the White House conference, eighteen "special concerns" groups met to discuss these and other neglected issues of the aged. There was general and vigorous agreement among delegates that lack of adequate income constituted the greatest crisis for the old. More than 4.7 million people over sixty-five were living below the poverty line. Pension fraud was rampant. Only 9 percent of the workers enrolled in private pension plans were actually receiving what they expected on retirement.

The White House conference culminated with a speech by Nixon, who proposed allocating an astonishing $100 million to a new nutrition program for the elderly. Despite our complaints, the conference was a turning point, drawing unprecedented national attention to the problems of the old.

Not long after, I participated in a panel discussion on changing family patterns on WPIX-TV in New York. I took a taxi to the television station with Reuben Gums, the producer of the show. I remember speaking to him about our Consultation of Older Persons and my experience at the White House gates. He said, "You know, that name doesn't sound like what you have in mind. I think you should call it the Gray Panthers."

I doubled over in laughter. "That's marvelous," I said. When I got home, I called up my friends and proposed the change. The majority endorsed the new name. It differentiated us from the other large, highly visible organizations for the old. Many of us felt strongly that we wanted to go beyond the national groups for "senior citizens" that had already been established, the highly successful American Association of Retired Persons and the National Council of Senior Citizens. These organizations, we felt, didn't encourage older people to take control of their lives or to concern themselves with larger social issues. Fighting for services and privileges for their members, many organizations for the old fell into the special-interest pit, as if the old were saying, "We worked damned hard and we're going to get ours."

Our new name gave us a sense of urgency, and after all, we did want to create a stir. Of course, some people misunderstood. A woman from Columbus, South Carolina, later wrote to us: "I was afraid at first to join your group (as I am sure many other people are) because I want to fight for our rights through our voting power and the name panthers frightened me because I don't want to become involved with bombings."

One of our early organizers, Margaret Hummel, was on the board of the Tabernacle Church in West Philadelphia. The pastor called her one day and offered a room in the church's basement for our group. It was the janitor's broom closet. I remember the pastor saying, "We'll just clean this up and paint it and it will make a terrific office." We had not expected luxury suites.

Jonathan, the janitor, moved his mops and buckets out, and we moved in a desk, a filing cabinet, two chairs, and a telephone, hauling the furniture to the church in a station wagon. Soon we got hold of a typewriter and a hand-operated duplicator. We started writing newsletters. We named our trusty duplicator—which got ink all over our hands—Gussy. We had a little brown notebook in which we tried to keep track of our expenses. When the first donation came in for ten dollars, we added an "Income" column and celebrated.

At that time there were a number of senior citizens groups in Philadelphia that had been loosely organized into the Action Group for the Elderly. A Presbyterian minister, a friend of mine, was attempting to coordinate the group, but without much success. I felt he,

like many organizers, wasn't soliciting enough input
from his troops and I told him so. He said, "You get
them going." I said, "Give me four to six months."

I called a meeting of the different groups and initiated a discussion among the members about what they
wanted to accomplish. Several people were disturbed
by a series of muggings of elderly people returning
from their banks. On the third day of each month
when Social Security checks arrived, old people went
to the bank to cash them. Since many of them couldn't
afford to open checking accounts, they walked home
with wallets full of cash.

After much discussion we all decided to act. We
agreed we would approach the president of First Pennsylvania Banking and Trust Co., the largest bank in the
Philadelphia area, with our grievances. There was a
general feeling among us that, when you reach sixty-
five, banks tend to forget you.

We went to the bank officials and demanded three
privileges for the old: free checking accounts, free
money orders, and their homes as collateral for loans.
Many of the city's elderly were unable to obtain loans
to fix up their homes because they did not meet credit
insurance standards.

The bank was not amenable. "These little accounts are unprofitable and a nuisance," one bank
official told us.

I egged the group on. "Tell him 'senior citizens'
and little people built his bank," I told them. "We are
more than grandmothers. We are citizens who will
press for what is just."

On May 8 an elderly woman was killed and robbed of $309 at Eighth Street and Indiana Avenue after she cashed a check at a savings society. I appealed to Ralph Nader, who had taken an interest in the work of the Gray Panthers. In a great stroke of luck, Nader knew the chairman of First Pennsylvania and a meeting was arranged. On a hot day in June, three dozen old people gathered in the boardroom of First Pennsylvania. We were determined to get our way. There is something wonderfully exhilarating about standing up to the head of a powerful bank.

Just a few weeks later, the bank acceded to our demands. John Bunting, board chairman of the First Pennsylvania Banking and Trust Co., agreed to set up special check-drawing savings accounts for people over sixty-five. Older bank customers could pay some standard bills, such as utility bills, with checks and get at least four money orders a month free of charge. The bank also agreed to bend over backward to write loans to older members. We were elated. And the bank got great publicity.

Meanwhile, in May 1972 I had gone to the General Assembly of the United Presbyterian Church in Denver as a volunteer member of the Church's Commission on the Status of Women in Society and in the Church. I was there with a friend to staff the commission—only incidentally as a Gray Panther. One morning when we decided to sleep late and have our breakfast in our room, we received a call from Frank Heinz, the Church's publicity director. An important Assembly delegate had failed to show up at a press conference. "Could you come on down?" he asked.

"I'll be delighted to meet the press," I told Frank. "You want me to talk about what the women are doing?"

"No. Talk about those old folks," he said. I got dressed and hurried down to the press conference. By that time, we had our name—the Gray Panthers. The press asked a few questions and I began to talk—and talk and talk. About retirement, about "senior citizens," about nursing homes, about sex at seventy-five, about gray-haired activists picketing for justice, about young people who felt powerless. The reporters were intrigued and the press conference went on for an hour and a half. The next day the story was around the country: UPI, AP, the *New York Times*, the *Denver Post*, and the *Washington Post* all picked it up. It went to more than one hundred news organizations and I was invited to appear on NBC's *Today Show*, Mike Douglas, and Johnny Carson. From that day on, the phone in our little broom closet rang constantly.

CHAPTER 7

Slingshots

When Gerald Ford was president, I and a few other activists were invited to the White House to watch him sign a pension bill. The bill, the first federal regulation of company pension plans, left something to be desired, but I was honored to be summoned for the occasion and decided to attend. On the appointed day, we were all ushered into the Cabinet Room, where we sat around a big table. After the president made an opening statement, people vied for his attention. I raised my hand repeatedly in an effort to comment on the legislation. Finally, he noticed me. "And what have you to say, young lady?" he asked.

Forgetting my prepared statement, I said firmly, "Mr. President, I am not a young lady. I'm an old woman." He was a little flustered and so were the others around the table. But I just couldn't help reminding him that his words weren't a compliment. Old people are old.

There would be many similar scenes in the years ahead. Even skilled politicians who realized the old had become a political force to reckon with could not refrain from patronizing us. During the Carter presidency, I was asked to attend a reception in honor of the old by Rosalynn Carter, who had pledged to take on the problems of the aged. The event was billed as a chance for the First Lady to get to know the concerns of activists for the aged. The First Lady, whom I found to be gracious and unpretentious, had invited two thousand "senior citizens" to attend.

We were entertained by the American Association of Retired Persons Kitchen Band from Hanover, Pennsylvania. The group played a "zesty rendition" of "I'm Forever Blowing Bubbles" with soup ladles, vegetable strainers, and pots and pans. The women in the band wore long baby dresses and baby bonnets and the men wore little red derbies that kept slipping off their bald heads. Another visiting band played coffee-can drums and kazoos. I found the spectacle embarrassing.

"Who put you up to this nonsense?" I asked a few members of the band. "You couldn't have thought it up yourselves—not at your age." They merely looked puzzled.

Why are old people so often treated like children? In one of our early efforts to establish a patients' rights committee in a Philadelphia nursing home, the administrators of the home, unable to understand that we were taking their patients seriously, asked that our first project be to help the residents make Easter baskets. What the patients really needed was to gain a place at the board table where the decisions about their lives were made. They needed freedom, spending money, respect, and fresh vegetables—not Easter baskets!

I am often portrayed as a cute old lady by the press. They love to describe my ninety-five-pound physique, my half-moon bifocals, and my wispy bun. It is much harder for people to see the determination that lies beneath my sense of fun.

In 1972 there was an explosion of interest in the Gray Panthers, and the letters started pouring in. Piles of them. I remember opening my front door and seeing teetering stacks of envelopes in my foyer. They came from small towns in the Midwest and European cities, neighborhoods a few miles from my home and places I had never known. The world had come to my doorstep.

It was heartening to discover there were thousands who agreed with me and identified with our cause. They wanted to support us, help us, join us. The letters came from all kinds of people—"a retired gentleman in reduced circumstances in Honolulu," a six-year-old boy, a middle-aged social worker. A man from Mississippi wrote: "I want to save money for old people and I want to join. I'm against young people in the organization and I'm against the name. Keep out the blacks. You should charge a membership fee." (We advised him not to sign up.)

"I don't think I'll be konking off too soon and would like to make good use of my time while I'm here," wrote one sixty-eight-year-old woman from Ohio.

A sixty-six-year-old woman from Lancaster, Pennsylvania, described her "lust for life." "It is a time of life that is beautiful, a time for being our individual selves and expressing it," she said. "I can flirt with young men and they love it; I can speak out on any issue. My grandchildren come to me with problems for I have the time to listen and they do not receive criticism."

Whether they were written in barely legible hand-writing or typed on the best typewriters, there was much intelligence, wit, zest, and insight in many of those letters. They were proof of a great untapped resource and were all the encouragement I needed to devote myself to this new enterprise.

All the years that I had worked for the Presbyterians, I didn't hold a press conference or write anything that wasn't strictly in line with the expressed action of the General Assembly. Needless to say, it would have been improper to do otherwise. As word of the Gray Panthers spread, I was interviewed by dozens of news-papers and magazines and appeared on talk shows. I was asked to speak before professional associations and at colleges and conventions. All of a sudden, I had none of the former constraints. I was free to speak my mind—and believe me, I did.

Our little coalition set about forming a national grass-roots organization. In 1973 we opened eleven chapters—we called them "networks"—in New York City, Syracuse, Dayton, Denver, Chicago, San Fran-cisco, Santa Fe, and Washington, D.C. Whenever I was invited to speak someplace, I would do a little organizing on the side. After a conference in Los An-geles, a group of students from the University of Southern Califorina, some older local activists, and a

Presbyterian minister convened in my hotel room. People were sitting everywhere—on beds, dressers, desks, and window sills. The Los Angeles network came to be known as "the bedroom group."

Many of us had spent our careers in large organizations and sometimes had felt constrained by the bureaucratic structure. We wanted an organization that would be loose and flexible. We had great faith in the grass roots, in the spirit and autonomy of our individual chapters. We did establish a national steering committee, but if you were looking for a formal structure, you'd need a microscope to find it. We wanted absolutely no hierarchy. We devised new language, referring to "conveners" instead of "chairpeople," "networks" instead of "chapters," and "articles of agreement" instead of "bylaws."

In 1972 Ralph Nader had started an organization, the Retired Professional Action Group, with similar goals. The idea was to hire retired people as employees and volunteers to work on social action projects. The organization received seven hundred applications from retired professionals for its twelve voluntary positions.

I met with Nader, whom I had long admired for his persistence and vision, to discuss our efforts. In 1973 Nader expressed an interest in merging his group with ours and asked me to move to Washington and head the new organization. The invitation was tempting, but I couldn't leave Sam in Philadelphia. His health was deteriorating and I needed to be close to him when I wasn't traveling.

Instead, Nader moved his organization to Philadelphia, to the basement of my house. His one staff member, Elma Holder, drove up one day with all the
organization's files. Nader's group, along with members of the Gray Panthers, had just completed a reveal-
ing investigation of the hearing-aid industry and issued
a scathing report, "Paying Through the Ear." Our
research showed that untrained and unqualified salesmen were conducting hearing tests and selling hearing
aids, frequently overdiagnosing hearing problems. As
part of the study, five Gray Panthers in New York City
were given hearing tests by a reputable audiologist and
were all found to have good hearing. They then visited
a few hearing-aid salesmen, with their first visit to one
near Columbia University, who prescribed hearing
aids for all of them. "Paying Through the Ear" re-
sulted in new federal regulations of the hearing-aid
industry.

Nader gave $25,000 to the newly enlarged Gray
Panthers. Elma Holder, an unassuming young woman
in her early thirties who was one of the most dogged
activists I had ever met, set up her office in the basement of my house and came to live with me. Soon
after, Linda Horn, a young nurse from Davenport,
Iowa, moved in to work with Elma on a citizen's action manual on nursing home reform. There were papers, books, files everywhere and our days were like
ongoing seminars. We would stay up into the early
morning hours discussing our work or addressing copies of the Gray Panthers newsletter.

The Gray Panthers still had its main office at the

Tabernacle Church, but had outgrown the janitor's closet and moved into the assembly room. High school and college students worked at the office as volunteers, answering the phone, opening the mail, and helping with the newsletter. I'll never forget their dedication. It made me realize how seldom high school students are given responsibility and a job to do. They were thrilled that we took them seriously.

I remember one high school student in particular, Matt Levy. One day he received a letter from a couple in the Midwest that was trying to reach a friend of theirs in a Philadelphia nursing home. Matt went to the nursing home and tracked down the woman, who was very infirm. He helped her write a letter back to her friends.

We received a few small grants and were able to hire one and then two full-time staff members. By 1974 we had Gray Panther groups in most of the major cities and many smaller ones, places such as Pasadena, California; Decatur, Illinois; Augusta, Georgia; and Madison, Wisconsin. They were working on dozens of different issues, including health care, nursing homes, public transportation, voter registration, housing, and legal services for the poor.

Our Denver group was successful in getting the city to extend crossing time at traffic lights by twenty-five seconds. The Philadelphia network began to pressure area colleges and universities to accept more older students. The Brooklyn Gray Panthers led efforts to prevent one hundred people from being evicted from a sixty-unit apartment building. And in

Los Angeles, the Gray Panthers set up a "tent city" downtown to protest the high cost of housing and its effect on people of all age groups.

In the '70s, the body of literature on the isolation, rejection, and low self-esteem of the old was growing. "The extended life expectancy has reduced the already limited social status of the old," wrote Dr. Robert Butler in his book *Why Survive? Being Old in America*. "Older people are commonplace among us, rather than unusual. Longevity is no longer viewed with awe and envy, now that it has been mass-produced through medical science."

Butler, who went on to become the head of the National Institute on Aging and a great friend of mine, was the first psychiatrist to describe the pervasive myths about old age, including that all old people are alike. *Why Survive?* won a Pulitzer prize in 1975.

In the tradition of the women's liberation movement, the common mission of all the Gray Panther groups was consciousness-raising. Instead of sexism, we were discovering "ageism"—the segregation, stereotyping, and stigmatizing of people on the basis of age. We brought new members together to exchange thoughts in weekly or monthly discussion sessions. Many of those who attended felt bereft and lonely in their old age but had never shared these feelings with anyone. As Viola Dudley, a San Diego Gray Panther, said, "Some of my friends and I feel that the years of living and learning which we consider of great value are not bearing fruit—for lack of knowing where to find fertile ground." People talked about their desire to work, about unwanted detachment from friends and children, about their hopes for the world. They felt demeaned and demoralized by the way they were treated in stores, on the street, in doctors' offices and in golden-age clubs.

Many of the people at those early meetings would smile sheepishly or respond with a wisecrack when asked their age. "You're as young as you feel!" they would say, embarrassed to admit how old they actually were. Remarks like this indicate how deeply we have been conditioned to hate our true selves, to reject our own bodies with the passage of time.

As we talked, we realized that old age isn't a disease, that we still had a great deal to offer the world. But if we were going to be liberated from the myth that old people are childlike, we must assert ourselves. We also said that we lived in a fast-paced, exploitive culture that was wasteful of vital human resources.

Simone de Beauvoir's book *The Coming of Age*, published in this country in 1972, was one of the most powerful statements on the neglect and disenfranchisement of the old. It strongly influenced my thinking and my goals in old age. "Society looks upon old age as a kind of shameful secret that it is unseemly to mention," wrote de Beauvoir.

> There is a copious literature dealing with women, with children, and with young people in all their aspects; but apart from specialized works, we scarcely find any reference whatsoever to the old. A French comic strip artist

once had to redraw a whole series because he had included a pair of grandparents among his characters. "Cut out the old folks," he was ordered. When I say that I am working on a study of old age, people generally exclaim, "What an extraordinary notion! . . . But you aren't old! . . . What a dismal subject.

While working on *The Coming of Age*, she wrote, "Great numbers of people, particularly old people, told me, kindly or angrily, but always at great length and again and again, that old age simply did not exist! There were some who were less young than others and that was all it amounted to."

We didn't limit our consciousness-raising to the old. Many of our new members were young or middle-aged. The subject of age affects everyone. All of us are aging and most of us will be old someday. It is such a simple concept, and yet it is something that so many people do not grasp until they are old.

In our competitive, profit-centered society, we have violated the essential wholeness of the life span, chopping it into segments each quite separate from the other.

We were deeply disturbed by the growing segregation of the old. Services in senior centers and meal sites under the Older Americans Act and federal housing programs for the old, though well-intentioned, had segregated the old from other age groups. Retirement communities, nursing homes, increased mobility, the entry of large numbers of women into the workforce—all had created a physical and emotional distance between the young and old. More and more grandchildren did not know their grandparents or, in fact, any old person well. To the young, old age had become an abstraction. A friend of mine went to speak before a group of elementary school children. "Where do old people come from?" she asked them. A child answered, "They're born from other old people."

There are college students who have never known an old person and who study topics like World War II and the Depression through textbooks only. There are nursing home residents who cry to see a child and busy adults who come across children or old people only on the street. How many of us really talk to old people about their lives before we ourselves become old?

In the 1970s the Gray Panthers were deeply alarmed that members of the burgeoning field of gerontology looked upon the separation of the old— from work, from families, from communities—as a normal part of life. According to the "disengagement theory," a prevailing view of aging that arose in the '60s, old age brings about a mutual withdrawal between the individual and society. According to the theory, the detachment and isolation many of the old feel is an inevitable and necessary prelude to death.

So often, gerontologists assumed that the intellectual and emotional deterioration of the aged are inevitable, ignoring the social and economic factors that precipitate it. The old were seen by gerontologists as problems to society, rather than as persons experiencing problems created by society. Public issues and controversies, thus reduced to private problems and complaints, were believed best dealt with by a social service system. Unfortunately, so many social service programs increased the dependency and powerlessness of the old.

I became convinced that gerontologists, viewing us as mere guinea pigs, had a vested interest in maintaining the illusion that people become incapacitated by age. Government dollars flowed to researchers who documented this illusion and to service providers who sustained it. Furthermore, certification of teachers and practicing gerontologists was accomplished through a system that overemphasized academic requirements and virtually ignored practical experience. Older people themselves were underused as resources, consultants, and experts in the field.

There was an urgent need for new research methods, which would explore the interaction between the individual and society and examine the diverse experiences of old people. Over the years I was engaged in a running feud with the American Gerontological Society that culminated in a debate at their annual conference in 1978 in San Francisco with George Maddox, the society's president that year. Before a packed auditorium in San Francisco, I urged the society to take stands on public issues—a new socialized health-care system, affordable shared housing, elimination of mandatory retirement. "We look for some awareness on the part of [gerontologists] of the social questions they ask, and a genuine concern for the nature and shape of our future," I said. There was applause for my ideas in some sections of the audience and strong disagreement in others.

"There is . . . a natural source of tension between advocates and scientists," Maddox retorted. "The Gerontological Society is primarily dedicated to research in aging; the Gray Panthers are primarily dedicated to restructuring the social order. . . . It is not obvious, at least not to me, that a primary dedication to advocacy or to science on the part of any particular individual or organization is morally superior or effective in achieving social change."

But I believed it was crucial that we demand some accountability from the scientists and researchers who influence our lives. We felt the medical establishment was one of the biggest offenders. Before the session closed, I gave George Maddox a Gray Panther T-shirt with our slogan "Age and Youth in Action." Maddox pulled it on and hugged me.

There was another momentous moment in San Francisco when I was invited by Professor Carroll Estes to address her class at the School of Nursing of the University of California. She had been researching the burgeoning gerontological field and the proliferation of public and private services for old people. Her book *The Aging Enterprise*, published by Jossy Bass, was the first of a lively, significant critique of America's response to "the demographic revolution." As a scholar and teacher, Estes established the Institute on Health and Aging, which has highlighted the urgent need for health care in late life. Carroll Estes and I have become loving friends and advocates for change. Her husband, Philip Lee, M.D., has been influential in health policy analysis for many years.

Early on, the Gray Panthers believed the health system was in crisis—a crisis that affected all age groups. Concern over the "bottom line" had replaced the Hippocratic oath.

The public debate over health care for the old began in the 1950s, and over the next two decades, a number of programs were established that promised to solve some of the problems, particularly the inability of the elderly to pay for rising medical costs. This periodic raising of expectations had its culmination in 1966 when, with the passage of Medicare, the nation's elderly were told they were finally going to get good health care. While Medicare was an effective treatment, it wasn't a cure.

The problem wasn't just high medical bills. We found that even the best health care for the old was often woefully inadequate. The ailments of the elderly were—and still are—often treated by a score of specialists who never communicate with each other. Factors that hinder the healing process, such as stress and disorientation, are often ignored, and the older patient is often viewed as a hypochondriac because of the frequency of his or her complaints.

As the Gray Panthers studied the issue, we were appalled that the nation's medical schools devoted little attention to the aging process. The training of physicians focused on acute illness, with little attention to chronic conditions in old age. According to the *New York Times*, in 1978 only 15 of the 20,000 faculty members at the country's medical schools specialized in geriatrics. Furthermore, the American Medical Association, which shapes the attitudes of millions of doctors, had provided no impetus for change. The AMA says, "The prime object of the medical profession is to render service to humanity," but it has traditionally guarded its own interests best.

In 1973 the AMA published "Health Hints for Older Americans," which offered such useful information as, "You can rid yourself of stomach gas by belching and intestinal gas by breaking wind," or "Constipation is one result of not chewing your food," or "Coughing is often present with a cold and usually stops as the cold improves." Big news to people who have lived for more than six decades.

The old did indeed have a need for health education. But what we needed to learn was how to deal effectively with physicians who treat us inhumanely and how to manage in a health care system that fails to address or meet the needs of our society. We needed to know how to live with chronic diseases and disabilities, how to achieve death with dignity, how to find home health care services, how to obtain medical assistance when Medicare and personal funds do not cover the expenses, how to arrange transportation to and from medical services.

At the 123rd Annual AMA Convention in Chicago in 1974, we challenged the AMA with specific demands: mandatory geriatric courses in medical schools, consumer representation in the association's House of Delegates, improved home care, cooperation in lifting Medicare restrictions, and help developing alternatives to nursing homes. With nurses, medical students, the Brothers of the Poor, a group of elderly Sisters of Mercy, and some physicians from Kansas City, we staged a picket line at high noon in front of the convention at the Palmer House in Chicago, where the AMA delegates were staying. On the front steps of the hotel, we engaged in guerrilla theater, with some of us dressed up as doctors and nurses trying to resuscitate a comatose AMA. One of our Chicago Panthers, dressed in a hospital gown labeled "Sick AMA," was laid out on a stretcher in the Palmer House lobby. A first-aid team carried him to the curb, where an ambulance, graciously provided by the Sisters of Mercy, was waiting. The team tried oxygen, mouth-to-mouth resuscitation, and, finally, deep chest massage. Vital signs returned only after the teams removed big wads of paper money from the chest cavity.

We didn't just press our point on the front steps. I had secured a press pass and I walked right into the auditorium where the AMA's House of Delegates was assembled. I marched up the aisle to the podium, where Dr. Russell B. Roth, the president of the AMA, was speaking. "Mr. Chairman," I said, waving my hand. "I have a letter to the House of Delegates from the Gray Panthers." I trembled as a hundred pairs of eyes glared at me. Dr. Roth left his place to personally escort me off the stage and toward the door.

I like to think my fearlessness was not without

effect. On the way out, a few doctors stopped to talk to me, displaying some interest in what I had to say, and we held a great press conference on the front steps of the Palmer House.

Go to the people at the top—that is my advice to anyone who wants to change the system, any system. Don't moan and groan with like-minded souls. Don't write letters or place a few phone calls and then sit back and wait. Leave safety behind. Put your body on the line. Stand before the people you fear and speak your mind—even if your voice shakes. When you least expect it, someone may actually listen to what you have to say. Well-aimed slingshots can topple giants.

And do your homework. In the '70s, when the Gray Panthers first appeared before Senate committees, national organizations, and the press, we always tried to document our complaints and recommendations. We didn't have the secretaries and fancy office equipment we had had during our "working" lives, but we had a great passion for our subject.

Many of us were disturbed that so much of what the young knew of the old was coming from television. What a disaster! Television portrayed the old as senile, dithering and incontinent.

Old people were never seen in commercials, unless they were hawking dentures or laxatives. They frequently were shown wearing turn-of-the-century clothing. An older character was never portrayed as sexually attractive or passionately in love—unless as a joke. In television dramas we were depicted as serene sages preoccupied with the past. Our voices high-pitched and querulous, we were shown as stubborn, rigid, forgetful, and confused. At the same time, news and documentaries played up the disaster and disease of old age, highlighting nursing homes and medical problems.

A study at the University of Pennsylvania's Annenberg School of Communications found that the old comprised less than 5 percent of the 2,741 characters in prime-time network dramas between 1969 and 1971 and that when they did appear they were usually villains or victims. The comedy skits of Dick Van Dyke, Carol Burnett, and Johnny Carson made me livid. Carson's "Aunt Blabby," Van Dyke's tripping geezer, and Burnett's toothless, stooped old woman—all were doddering fools. As Jeanne Schallon, a Los Angeles Gray Panther, told the *New York Times* in 1977, "I'm sixty-two, my mind never worked better, but when I take a prescription to the druggist, he treats me like an imbecile child. That's the way television has taught him to treat me."

We weren't the only organization concerned about the problem. The National Council on Aging set up an office in Hollywood in 1976 and hired two people to monitor television programs for how they portray the aging. The staffers offered a hot-line for writers who needed advice on how to include older characters in scripts. Helyne Landres, the head of the office, told the *Times* that the writers who called her

"sometimes sound as though [they're] seeking guid-
ance on the life-styles of some fragile, alien culture."
One writer said he was thinking of creating a scene
calling for a roomful of older folks and wondered if a
doctor would have to be on the set. Another was
curious if an eighty-year-old could possibly rob a
bank. Definitely yes, he was told. But, Mrs. Landres
added, "please make it clear he was always a bank
robber."

Heleyn Landres tried to get older contestants on
the game shows. As she told the *Times*, she spoke "to
every game show producer in town and every one
resists. One young woman said, 'Oh, all right, you can
bring some of your old people down here and they can
watch.' I said, 'They don't want to watch, they want to
be contestants.' She acted as though it were the most
idiotic request she had ever heard. 'We can't use old
people. They're all senile, they talk too much, they're
too slow.' "

I remember the first time I was on Johnny Carson
in 1974. I think Carson probably intended to make
fun of me—you know, Grandma Moses takes on the
world. But I have learned that on talk shows you have
to take initiative. Before Johnny could question me, I
leaned forward and said, in a beguiling tone, "Johnny,
I'm so glad you don't dye your hair. Your gray hair is
becoming." He was flustered and pleased. He
smoothed his hair, straightened his tie, and smiled.

In 1974 we formed television monitoring groups.
Lydia Bragger, a member of our New York City
group, was the leader of this effort. Lydia had had a

career in public relations and was extremely effective in getting our message across. Lydia set up regular schedules for her Media Watch, and enlisted other Media Watchers in other cities. When she approached TV managers with a particular complaint she spoke with conviction and charm and documented her observations with files of statistics and facts.

In 1975 Lydia and I wrote a letter of protest to Arthur Taylor, then president of CBS, about pervasive put-downs of the old on TV. Within two weeks we received a phone call from the network arranging a meeting with Thomas Swafford, a CBS vice president. As a result of our meeting with Mr. Swafford, we met with the National Association of Broadcasters on April 30, 1975, in Washington.

We requested that age be added to the topics— race, sex, creed, and color—that the NAB code said should be treated with sensitivity. We used blow-ups, film segments, and transcripts to document our complaints. The addition was considered by the NAB and approved a few months later. In December 1975, the Gray Panthers convened a weekend conference in New York on "The Media and Age" with CBS producers, writers, editors, and program releasers. The report of that conference generated a lot of soul-searching and change.

My house in those years was paved with paperwork—I had a clear path only to the bathroom and bedroom. I restricted my travel somewhat to stay near my brother, who still needed a great deal of care. He was not well—either physically or emotionally. He had become obese and incontinent and would sit for days in the same purple bathrobe in a chair in his bedroom, rising only to eat.

I never invited guests to the house because I couldn't predict what Sam would say or do. He sometimes yelled at people on the phone and he was prone to fits of anger, then depression. Once, when we were discussing my plans to travel, he became enraged and grabbed a knife in the kitchen. He raised it above his head as if he were going to lunge at me. I was very frightened but kept calm. "Put it down, Sam. I won't go away. Please, put it down." He put it down immediately and rushed to his room.

For a time, I took every opportunity I could to think about other things. I saw to my brother's care, but remained active in my work. My housemates, Elma and Linda, were wonderfully compassionate and understanding. Through close, daily contact with him, they came to understand him and could brush aside his tantrums and broodings. Six teenage boys from the neighborhood were also his friends. They came by after school to talk to Sam and to play chess and checkers. They were a blessing.

In 1975 Sam's condition deteriorated further. A hernia caused his scrotum to enlarge to the point where he walked with difficulty and could not wear pants or lie down to sleep. Still he refused to go to a doctor. A psychiatrist friend agreed to come to the house to examine him. She said surgery was critical to his survival and agreed he should no longer remain at home. She talked to him for more than an hour and somehow—how I will never know—convinced him to go to a psychiatric hospital, where she hoped he would be persuaded to consent to an operation on his hernia.

When the day came, he did not leave willingly. I had arranged for him to go to a private hospital. When a policeman came to the house to help take him away, he began to cry and screamed, "What have you done to me? What would Mother say? You promised you would take care of me." I pleaded with him. "Sam, this is to get you well," I said. "It's to take care of your health. This is the only way we can make you better." He was a pathetic sight. Sending him away was the hardest thing I have ever done.

At the psychiatric hospital, they counseled him and prepared him for admission to Chestnut Hill Hospital. After the operation, which at first appeared to have gone well, he went to a rehabilitation hospital in Center City. But he had developed a massive staphylococcus infection and became gravely ill. He was transferred to yet another hospital and put in intensive isolation. When I visited him, I wore a hospital gown and a mask to protect him from further infection.

His heart and kidneys began to fail. Twice his heart stopped and the doctors resuscitated him. Though they brought him back to life, he remained comatose much of the time. One day, after he had spent ten days in a coma, the doctors told me he would need to be put on dialysis to live and that they wanted my consent for the procedure. I went into his room and stood beside his bed. Looking at his wrecked and exhausted body and at the tubes that protruded from his mouth, I felt, in my heart and soul, that he was ready to die. His life was over whether they kept him technically alive or not.

I went to the head doctor in charge and told him I would not consent to the dialysis. Today such a decision, though still difficult and controversial, is perhaps a bit easier than it was back then when life-support machines were less common. I remember a doctor looking at me as if I were crazy. "You can save him!" he said. "He does not have to die!" I thought the doctors—who admitted that even with dialysis, Sam would be comatose—were the crazy ones. They would sustain his life only to make him suffer.

One of the doctors insisted I see the hospital psychiatrist. I was seeing a psychiatrist of my own at the time because I was so upset, but I went to the one on the hospital staff and explained my view. He agreed with me—and then sent me a bill for a hundred dollars.

I prayed constantly, asking the Creator to help me get through this hell. One day, after eating lunch in the hospital cafeteria, I walked into Sam's room to find the nurses loading him onto a stretcher to take him to dialysis. I looked at them squarely and said, "No, I have not approved that treatment. You cannot take him away." It took all of my courage to say it.

For the next few days, Elma, Linda, and I took turns at Sam's bedside. I can't imagine how I would have made it through that painful time without my friends. They supported my decision to let my brother die and helped me remain calm. Sam never regained consciousness; he died quietly within the week. Elma, Linda, and I were with him. We all felt at peace.

Five people attended his private funeral at First Presbyterian. The organist played Sam's favorite Bach cantata. His death was a great release—for him and for me. The day after his funeral, I went to Ohio to visit some friends. I got on the plane and haven't landed since.

For more than sixty years, I had devoted a part of myself to Sam. I had coached him, nursed him, comforted him, loved him, fought with him. It was a lonely burden that made me feel a great kinship with others who have brothers, sisters, sons, or daughters who are mentally ill. There is nothing more demanding and challenging.

Every day since Sam's death has been relatively joyous. I know I will never relive that kind of pain for I will never feel so intimately involved in another person's fate, so responsible for another's life. I'm impelled by that tragic experience to live my life to the fullest. On a wall in the upstairs hallway in my house, I keep a picture of the four of us—my mother, father, Sam, and me. We were all happy on that occasion. My mother is wearing my father's hat, Sam has a broad smile on his face, and my father and I appear to be laughing at some joke. That's how I like to remember us all.

CHAPTER 8

Friends and Foes

One day in 1975, Elma Holder, my co-worker and housemate, was working in the basement office in my house when she received a telephone call from an official of the American Health Care Association, the trade group for nursing home operators. The man proudly announced that the association—for the first time in its history—was going to invite consumer advocates to a meeting with its members. The topic of the meeting would be "participatory management" of nursing homes.

The man told Elma they were going to start off slowly, inviting just eight representatives from the Gray Panthers and eight from the American Association of Retired Persons. Elma asked him, "But why don't you invite the thirty groups we're in contact with all over the country?" He instantly opposed the idea.

Elma—a real wolf in sheep's clothing—said, "Look, these people will never be able to come anyway. They don't have the money to fly. Just invite them. It would be a nice gesture." Somehow, after much hedging, he was persuaded. Elma hung up and we immediately got on the phone to everybody we knew who was interested in nursing home reform. "This is our big chance to meet each other," we told them.

The conference was going to be held in Washington, D.C. We convinced the nursing home association to give us a room a day early. Twelve of the thirty groups of citizen activists sent representatives, and we all got together and laid out our common concerns, things like nurse's-aide training, residents' rights committees, federal regulations. We decided then and there to form an ad hoc organization and call it the National Citizens Coalition for Nursing Home Reform.

We got more nervy and asked the nursing home operators if they could set aside a room for us the next day so we could hold a press conference. They were quite apprehensive at this point, but they agreed to do it. We stayed up all night and worked on a press release and got people on the telephone to call the media. Only one newspaper showed up—the *Baltimore Sun*—but we still felt overjoyed at the start of our new group. Our new movement.

Nursing home reform is hard and controversial work. It's not for sissies. By the early '70s, there had been a dramatic rise in the number of nursing homes—the result of an aging population, improvements in medical care, greater family mobility, and increasing acceptance of placing the aged and infirm in institutions—and they were making big bucks. Between 1960 and 1970, the number of nursing homes increased by 140 percent, the number of beds by 232 percent, and the number of patients by 210 percent. By 1974 over 1.2 million people were in nursing homes and one in five people over sixty-five was expected to spend some time in a nursing home. From 1969 through 1974, expenditures on nursing home fees increased by about 1,400 percent. What other businesses see this kind of growth in a decade!

With 80 percent of the nation's nursing homes operating for profit (only 13 percent of all hospitals did), concern mounted about the care provided in these institutions. There was a sudden rash of books about neglect and abuse of nursing home residents. Newspapers reported an escalating number of nursing home fires.

In the summer of 1971, substandard nursing homes were the central topic of a major address by President Nixon on the problems of the aged. Nixon announced an eight-point nursing home reform program including training of state nursing home inspectors, expansion of the federal enforcement program, and reduction of federal funds to facilities not meeting standards.

Three years later a Senate subcommittee on long-term care found the situation little improved. According to Senator Frank Moss, the subcommittee chairman, "Long-term care for older Americans stands today as the most troubled, and troublesome, component of our entire health care system." The subcommittee issued a report, "Nursing Home Care in the United States: A Failure in Public Policy," that

was the result of fifteen years of fact-finding, thirty-six
Senate hearings and about three hundred pages of testimony. It criticized past policies and programs as
"piecemeal, inappropriate, illusory and short-lived."

The nursing home industry's interests were protected by accomplished attorneys, lobbyists, and public relations firms. Government regulatory agencies,
on the other hand, were often understaffed and under-
financed. There was a crying need for citizen action.

The crisis in nursing home care was—and continues to be—a public issue. "We have made the decision
to entrust many of our older people—which is to say
ourselves—to nursing homes," wrote Mary Adelaide
Mendelson, author of *Tender Loving Greed*, the 1974
award-winning examination of abuse in nursing
homes. "The nursing homes have failed horribly in
that trust. But, the blame in a profit-making society
cannot all be laid at their door. . . . The government
also has failed. Yet, if the government belongs to us,
we share the failure with the bureaucrats."

Billions of dollars in federal funds are poured
every month into the nursing home industry through
Medicare and Medicaid payments. Almost half of all
nursing home costs, about $21.5 billion a year, are
publicly financed. Furthermore, any of us—no matter
what age we are or how wealthy we are—could someday end up in a nursing home. We all have a stake in
the system that oversees these institutions.

Yet few nursing homes are an active part of a larger
community. Elma Holder became interested in nursing homes when she was in high school in Tulsa, Okla-

homa, and started visiting a longtime neighbor who
had moved to a home. She would visit Mrs. Craig
every week and take her to a restaurant. She couldn't
understand why no one else in the neighborhood
showed Mrs. Craig attention after she moved to the
home. Therein lies so much of the problem. People
are afraid of visiting nursing homes, seeing in them an
unhappy picture of what their own future might hold
or feeling guilt for having put their own relatives in
homes. Instead of letting their frustrations serve a con-
structive purpose—nursing home reform—they avoid
these institutions and the segregation of nursing home
residents is intensified.

Many of us in the Gray Panthers worked to encourage home health care and other alternatives to
nursing homes, fervently believing that there are many
people in nursing homes who don't need to be there.
At the same time, we fought for change within institutions because good nursing home care must be available for those who need it.

We first set our sights on organizing nursing home
residents, the vast majority of whom seemed not to
know what their money should buy or what services
they should expect. Many of the residents were bored,
lonely, and apathetic. In many ways this was more
distressing than problems like poor food or the short-
age of nurses. It is a commonly believed myth that
nursing home residents are compliant victims who
cannot fend for themselves. I believe even weak, isolated members of society can affirm their rights. Nursing home residents can be encouraged—with

community support—to come out of their shells. Starting in a nursing home in West Philadelphia and expanding to institutions around the country, the Gray Panthers tried to offer that support.

I will never forget the fight three hundred residents of a San Francisco home put up when the state threatened to close the institution. We like to call the Post Street rebellion the first uprising of nursing home residents in this country.

In 1978 the San Franciscan Convalescent Center on Post Street was home to three hundred of the city's elderly poor. It was a good place for a nursing home— in the heart of the city, where the patients were close to friends and families. It has always saddened me to see nursing homes in cornfields or isolated suburban tracts. They should be in the thick of things so that visitors can get to them and able residents can come and go.

The San Franciscan was plagued by financial problems that its operators blamed on the inadequacy of payments under Medi-Cal, the state's health insurance program. The home was receiving about twenty-seven dollars per day for each patient, which might have been realistic in less expensive parts of California, but wasn't in line with the cost of living in San Francisco. In 1977 the state Department of Health revoked the San Franciscan's license because of minor health code violations that the local Gray Panthers believed could have been easily corrected. The real problem, we believed, was the lack of funds.

The state was preparing to transfer the patients to

homes outside the city—some of which were hundreds of miles away—when the unexpected occurred. A few of the patients courageously decided to fight to stay. Though they depended on the state and the home for everything, they took a stand.

At a press conference called by the residents, eighty-six-year-old Mary Baldwin read a statement through a magnifying glass. She announced their resolve to "remain with our friends and near our loved ones." The residents had contacted the local Gray Panthers, who in turn hired public interest lawyers to file a suit against the state for more money for the home.

The Gray Panthers staged sit-ins at Governor Jerry Brown's office and spent a day following him around, hoping to convince him to visit the San Franciscan and talk to the residents himself. Brown finally agreed to visit the home. He spent about thirty minutes on Post Street, but later he still refused to provide higher Medi-Cal payments. In July the residents were wheeled out, many of them weeping, and taken to homes outside the city. More than half of them died within eight months of leaving the home.

As the nursing home business grew, reform efforts began to spring up in different parts of the country—often the result of fearless action on the part of lone individuals. For example, the organization Kansans for the Improvement of Nursing Homes was the result of a one-woman crusade by Petey Cerf, who became a Red Cross volunteer in a nursing home in the 1950s. Explaining her work in *Nursing Homes: A Citizens Action Guide*, written by Elma Holder and Linda Horn in my home, she said that she was so shocked by the conditions in one nursing home that she persuaded three nurse's aides to sign affidavits describing the problems in the home. She ultimately succeeded in closing the institution.

Her story is typical: many nursing home activists are women, moved to take action after visiting nursing homes. Marion Ballentine, a retired schoolteacher in Spokane, Washington, began a local chapter of Citizens for the Improvement of Nursing Homes after she met a fifty-five-year-old woman who worked as a nurse's aide in a nursing home for two dollars an hour and no benefits. When the aide attempted to commit suicide, presumably because of her working conditions, Mrs. Ballentine started a campaign to unionize local nursing home employees.

Nursing homes, I believe, are a feminist issue. Because women outlive men by an average of eight years, the vast majority of nursing home residents are women. Also, so many of the underpaid and poorly trained aides in nursing homes are women. Their deplorable working conditions are the root of much of the problem.

The National Citizens Coalition for Nursing Home Reform—a joint venture of the various reform groups that we brought together in Washington—began to present its views and to counterbalance the power of the nursing home trade associations. The organization was a major force behind passage of the 1987 Nursing Home Reform Law, which ensures that the status of every nursing home resident is regularly reviewed and that his or her rights are maintained. Elma heads the organization, which now has three hundred member groups and an office in Washington; she makes ongoing strides in its work. Her advocacy has changed nursing home care in America.

After my brother died, I no longer restricted my travel, logging more than 100,000 miles in 1976. Sometimes I was a little dazed by my schedule. I remember the time I attempted to catch a flight home after a speaking engagement in Minnesota. A student drove me into the Minneapolis airport in her Volkswagen during a blizzard, depositing me, safe but weary, at the airport.

When I sat down to wait for my flight, the airport was crowded with people and I began to doze. When I opened my eyes, the waiting area was empty. In a panic I rushed out to catch my plane. The airline officials let me through without checking my ticket or boarding pass. As the plane started down the runway, I heard the captain's voice over the intercom: "Welcome . . . We hope you have a good trip *west*." I was heading for San Francisco, not Philadelphia.

My life on the road taught me some tough lessons.

In 1977, I was in Washington for a meeting and a visit with friends. My friend, Paul Nathanson, had picked me up at my hotel and taken me to a meeting. Afterward, he drove me back to the hotel, dropping me off at the curb because it was very difficult to park. When I ran in to get my key, there was somebody sitting in the lobby, a well-dressed white man in his late twenties or early thirties. He stood up and got in the elevator with me. I didn't think anything of it, of course.

When I got to my floor, I left the elevator and walked a long distance to my room, along a corridor with all sorts of twists and turns. It seemed an interminable walk. As I put my key into the door, I heard a muffled sound behind me. I turned around to see the man from the elevator looming behind me. Grabbing me by the arm, he pushed open the door and forced me into the room. It happened so quickly, I didn't have time to scream. I was stunned.

He pushed me onto the bed and pulled off all my clothes. His moves were so forceful, so violent, I didn't think to resist in any way. I was certain he was going to rape me. He pulled my panty hose down over my face so that I could barely see. I heard him searching my handbag and my wallet. There was a pause while he looked at the contents of my wallet, which contained only a few dollars, and then I heard him say, "I'm leaving now." I gasped.

But before he left, he pulled me up and pushed me into the bathroom. As I crouched on the cold tile floor, he turned on the bathwater. I thought he was going to drown me. I felt my heart almost stop—perhaps it did stop. "I'm going to New York," he said. "You'll never find me."

He walked out of the bathroom and then I heard the door to my room slam behind him. I stayed on the floor for a few minutes, afraid to move and uncertain whether he had truly left. Finally, I struggled to the phone and called the front desk. There was a great to-do, of course. The police came and took finger-prints and interviewed me extensively. Paul, my friend, was especially troubled, as if he had been re-sponsible.

I was shaken and weak for a few days. Mostly, I felt tremendously lucky. Why hadn't he attacked me? What had he intended to do? My guess is that he saw my identification in my wallet, perhaps recognized my name, and feared attacking someone known to the public. As far as I know, my attacker has never been arrested and I have often wondered whether he has stalked other women in lonely corridors. The incident did not make me a fearful woman, but I have never again ventured down a hotel corridor alone.

My health in those years didn't always cooperate with my schedule. In 1976 I had another bout with cancer. I received a notice from my gynecologist that a pap smear showed some abnormality. I ignored the notice, fearing a long-term bout with cancer that would involve chemotherapy. I dreaded that kind of thing.

However, my gynecologist called and said, "I re-ally do want to see you." My housemates urged me to be examined and I complied. The doctors found uter-ine cancer, which fortunately was not invasive. I recovered from a radical hysterectomy in record time! Six weeks and two days after the surgery, I attended the inauguration of President Jimmy Carter, whom I saw as a welcome change in the White House.

My Gray Panther friends and I did not sit around complaining about our ailments. We felt that our trials gave us personal perspective on the health system. A number of us had cancer and it was therapeutic to have so many friends who had triumphed—spiritually, at least—over this sickness. I remember the time Lillian Rabinowitz, a member of our network in Berkeley, California, who was undergoing chemotherapy, came to my house with her special marijuana brownies—a popular remedy for the side effects of the treatment. The flutist in Lillian's baroque music group—Lillian played the piano—had suggested she try it.

Lillian initially dismissed the idea. However, a friend of the flutist appeared at Lillian's door one day with a small grocery bag filled with marijuana. Not sure what to do with the contents, Lillian tore up some of the leaves and put them in her salad. Nothing happened. She then went to a head shop in Berkeley for a pipe and instructions on how to smoke it. Still, nothing. She called her supplier. "Break up some leaves into a skillet," he instructed. "Brown them lightly in butter and then mix it all into a brownie batter and bake." Lillian took to making marijuana brownies on her bad days. One day she brought a batch to my house for a breakfast meeting. They were delicious—but, I can't say I found them very potent. Did we laugh more than usual—who knows?

In 1975 the Gray Panthers had its first national convention. The gathering really established us as a national organization—or movement, as we liked to call it. We were gradually introducing more structure into our freewheeling operation. By then we had a national steering committee, which held carefully planned meetings, with an agenda and official minutes.

I will never forget that convention in Chicago. There was gray hair, blond hair, hair down to the shoulders—all types of hair. Many of us felt like kids playing hooky—free from the strictures of our former lives. There were many university students among us. It was interesting to observe the contrast in decision-making styles. The young wanted to charge in on every issue and change the world in seven days. The older members had more patience. We struck a balance and demonstrated that we were "Age and Youth in Action."

We formally adopted a body of resolutions in a heated session that lasted well into the night as every last word was debated. At one point a delegate stood up and announced, "All of you passionate dedicated nitpickers shut up and sit down!" The final body of resolutions reflected the organizations' far-reaching and eclectic goals—reduction of military spending, a new health system, an end to compulsory retirement and age discrimination in employment, and new housing options for young and old. A Men's Liberation Caucus was formed and succeeded in getting passed a resolution calling for more involvement of men in the group. A resolution from the Youth Caucus to legalize marijuana aroused such strong feelings that opponents asked that votes be registered by name.

There were some disputes about our name. I remember an older woman snapping, "Why do we use the name Gray Panthers? One thinks of violence, drugs, murder, the overthrow of existing regimes." But, by and large, our name seemed to fit us and our feistiness. I felt part of a community of like-minded souls.

Many of our members were first generation immigrants, or the children of first generation immigrants, who had fled Europe to escape political or religious repression. Because those experiences were so close to them, they valued democracy. They were activists to the bone. Many had worked in the progressive movements of the '30s and '40s, the trade unions and churches and social action organizations. I always loved to hear the stories of the people drawn to our organizations.

At the age of sixteen, Anne McDougall, a member of our Los Angeles group, was threatened with expulsion from Central High School in Birmingham, Alabama, after she argued in a debate that utilities should be publicly owned. She became a journeyman welder during World War II and, later, a secretary. At the age of fifty-three, she became a licensed nurse and worked for another twenty years. "I've never learned how to do nothing," I recall her saying in her late seventies. "I don't feel any particular age, but sometimes I have to stop and remember that my son is now a senior citizen."

During the Depression Chuck Preston, the editor of our newspaper, *The Network*, sold Christmas cards in his college dancing shoes, a piece of cardboard covering a hole in one of the soles. He got his start as a "radical" when he attended a meeting of the John Reed Club, a network of leftist artists and writers. "From that moment on I was a Red," he always liked to say. Chuck wrote for the *Pulse of the Nation*, a newspaper out of Indianapolis, and then other left-wing publications. In every encounter, letter, or phone call with Chuck, you couldn't escape a pitch. Even "Merry Christmas" was followed by ". . . and save Social Security."

When Dr. Irvin Portner retired from his medical practice in Boston, he moved to Sarasota, Florida, where he became a member of our local network. Not wanting to spend all his retirement on the golf course, and feeling there was a great need for free medical care for Sarasota's poor elderly, he opened a health clinic. It was supported, in part, by funds from his former patients in Boston. The clinic grew to a staff of twenty doctors.

Many of us have been through great personal hardship—I think that is our strength as an organization. We were not defeatists but had a persistence born of experience. In 1969 Gregory Bergman, a member of our group in Berkeley, lost his wife in a car accident. He went into a deep depression and thought he would never find happiness again. But, as he discovered, as long as our minds are healthy, we are all capable of renewal—at any age. Over the next few years, Gregory came out of his shell. After having worked as a book-keeper for twenty-five years in a lumber mill in the Sierras east of Sacramento, Gregory moved to Berke-

ley and, in his mid-sixties, started a second career as a
writer and became a part-time graduate student in theology. He learned to dance to rock music and traveled
to Europe and South America for the first time. "I'm
in the mainstream of life in a serious way," he likes to
say. "Not up some side stream."

Lydia Bragger, one of our earliest members,
moved from Providence, Rhode Island, to New York
City at the age of sixty, after her husband died and her
children were grown. She was ready to try something
new.

Lydia, who favors black boots, flowing skirts, and
capes, started holding meetings of the Gray Panthers
in her apartment on the West Side of Manhattan. Her
roommates at Gray Panther conventions would awake
to find her standing on her head—part of her morning
exercise routine. She was also fond of chewing garlic—
her secret for a long life. At the age of eighty-five, she
completed her master's degree in gerontology at
Hunter College. She is now a radio talk show host on
WBAI.

So many people think the old are intractably set in
their ways, but my friends had proven that they were
capable of great personal change, even in their sixties,
seventies, and eighties. They were willing to explore
and experiment with new life-styles—taking college
degrees, having love affairs, joining the Peace Corps.

We were extremely curious about how people
aged in other countries. In 1978 I was asked by the
U.S.–China People's Friendship Association to lead a
study tour of the People's Republic of China. Twenty-
four of us, including several members in their twen-

ties, traveled to China to conduct our own informal study of old age in that country. On the flight from Los Angeles to Peking, we divided up into committees: health care, retirement, women, housing. Equipped with notebooks and several thousand questions, we weren't on vacation. At first, the tour guides were somewhat nonplussed by our request for meetings with lawyers and planners and visits to factories. But they complied and we saw a lot. I was fascinated by our visits to hospitals, where treatment is holistic. Medicines that have been used for nine hundred years are still prescribed. Hospital equipment was "primitive" in comparison with our hi-tech medical machines, but we found true healing.

I'll never forget our tour of the Home of Respect outside Shanghai, one of the few nursing homes in China. All was neat and well-tended. There were vegetable gardens and smiling retirees playing checkers. The sight of this bright, cheery institution was comforting to us. But we hesitated to make comparisons with the situation in our own country. Our tour was strictly controlled—we were given just a glimpse into the lives of the old in China.

Still, we concluded that the old are not as isolated in China as they are in this country. I remember Mrs. Chang, a fifty-nine-year-old resident of a neighborhood commune in Shanghai. She lived in a two-room apartment with her son, daughter-in-law, and grandchild. Mrs. Chang had retired from her work at a cotton mill at the age of fifty-five. In keeping with tradition, her fellow workers accompanied her home on her last day of work, singing songs and presenting her family with paper flowers. She spent her days marketing, taking her grandson to and from nursery school, taking classes, watching TV, and visiting friends.

Mrs. Chang seemed happy. Her way of life would not work for millions of Americans, who would not be happy baby-sitting, living in two-room apartments, and retiring at fifty-five. It was her usefulness, her sense of purpose, and her place at the center of a community that can serve as a model here.

Tour groups of Westerners were still relatively new then. Wherever we went in China, we were surrounded by crowds of curious onlookers. With my white hair and skin, I especially was a novelty. I remember rushing out of a department store in Peking one day because I was late getting back to the bus. A crowd of what seemed like hundreds of Chinese stood around the bus, staring at its occupants. When I emerged from the store, the throng parted like the Red Sea.

One day a member of our group left her pen on a counter in a bank in Changchun. About an hour or so later, in a crowded department store several miles away, a bank clerk caught up with us to return the pen. This small act of kindness astounded us.

My work with the Gray Panthers brought me great friendships. I remember the day in 1973 when I arrived at the airport in Portland, Oregon, to make a speech before a local group. A young man—he was eighteen—had come to pick me up in a sporty Datsun 240Z. He was an attractive, engaging man, a student at the University of Washington who had joined the local Gray Panthers. On the way into the city, we talked nonstop.

We maintained some casual contact over the next few years, until 1976 when I happened to be in San Francisco, where he was visiting his family. It was his twenty-first birthday and we arranged to have dinner together. We went to a Lebanese restaurant where we sat on the floor and ate with our fingers. There was a belly dancer who gyrated while we ate. My companion was a bit embarrassed when she came to our table, but I was not. I tucked a dollar into the woman's waist-band.

Our relationship became more than just a friendship. There was a fifty-year difference in our age, but there was a spark between us. When I saw him unclothed for the first time, he reminded me of the little bronze replica of a Greek god—a souvenir of a trip abroad—that sits on my night table.

Our relationship lasted for a year or so. We saw each other when we could. He started working in Washington, D.C., when he graduated and would come to Philadelphia to visit me. In time, we parted amicably. We had both known it wouldn't last forever, but it was a cherished experience for both of us.

Why is it that the pairing of an older man with a younger woman is approved of, while an older woman with a younger man is frowned upon? The 1971 movie *Harold and Maude* was a rare look at the subject, but

the film offended me. Harold was sick and Maude was
kooky. I didn't see why a normal, sane, average old
woman couldn't become involved with a normal
young man. It happened to me and it can happen to
others.

My affair shocked some older women who were
uptight and out of touch with their own sexual and
romantic feelings. "There's a lot older women can
offer younger men," I would say—and I believe it. I
think older women can help young men learn about
sexuality without making them feel they have to per-
form. Besides, many older women are attractive and
sensual—and young men don't go for just Barbie
dolls.

Our sexuality is so influential in determining who
we are and how we relate to others. Indeed, it is the
material of life and to deny it in old age is to deny life
itself. In old age we have the time and patience to
express our sexuality in various ways. I liked the
words of Bob Butler and Myrna Lewis in their book,
Sex After Sixty: "Make sex an art." Sexual satisfaction
is available to many people into advanced age. We are
learning more and more about the psychological as
well as physiological responses of old people. This is
an age of liberation.

Or is it? A few years back social work students at
Brandeis University were asked to complete the statement, "Sex for most old people is . . ." Words like
"negligible," "unimportant," a "thing of the past,"
were typical responses. Middle-aged adults are often
shocked to learn that their parents continue to enjoy

each other. The children of my peers are sometimes horrified, antagonistic, and bitter when their mothers or fathers seek to remarry or have a love affair. Old men and women who act on their normal sexual impulses in the privacy of their own bedrooms are considered perverse.

And, as Butler points out, "The average doctor does not think sex matters in old age." Thus, research and treatment of the often correctable sexual problems of the old remain tragically inadequate. Butler gives the example of a seventy-two-year-old man who asked his physician for help with his lessened potency just before he planned to remarry. He asked his doctor whether he could be given hormone pills or an injection that would help him. "The woman I'm going to marry is a wonderful person and I don't want to disappoint her," the man said. Instead of examining the man to see if anything could be done medically to aid him, the doctor dismissed the idea as not worth bothering about. "If she's a wonderful woman," he pontificated, "she'll understand."

Unfortunately, many old people themselves often believe their sexual feelings are unhealthy. This only adds to their isolation and depression. What a waste! In old age women should feel freer because they can enjoy sex without concern about pregnancy. Men should be free from the macho attitude that they always have to achieve full, quick erection. Prolonged sex play can give both partners pleasure and release from loneliness and tension.

I have known many people who have enjoyed sex

in their old age, not just the sex act itself—but all that surrounds it. They have enjoyed dancing and hugging and necking and writing love notes. A few years ago a friend of mine attended her fiftieth high school reunion in a small town in Minnesota. The first person she laid eyes upon when she walked into the reunion was her high school beau. She threw her arms around him and he said, "My, I've been waiting a long time for this." The two adjourned to her car in the parking lot, where they made love in the front seat—as they would have liked to have done years before in high school.

In old age, people no longer need to worry about finding the perfect mate. About fifteen years ago a dear friend of mine, a sixty-four-year-old divorcée who had been unhappily married to a scholar, went with a tour group to Japan. On her trip she met an engineer, a widower in his sixties. Though he was not the type of man she would have married, she was drawn to him.

In her younger days she would have waited for him to make an overture, but as soon as she returned from Japan she wrote the man a note asking him to take a photography course with her. Soon they were spending weekends together at his apartment in Northeast Philadelphia. Every Friday night they would drink beer and dance at a German taproom and then go back to his apartment. She enjoyed sex for the first time.

Two women friends of mine in their sixties became lovers. One was a divorcée, the other, a widow. They lived together in Berkeley, where they nursed each other through cancer. A few years back I suggested in a public speech that older women who cannot find male lovers because of the scarcity of older men should look to each other for love. The house practically came down on me! Sponsors threatened to withdraw support from the Gray Panthers. People scolded me, saying my remarks were in poor taste. I don't regret what I said. Unfortunately, there are many older women who, because of circumstance and convention, will not fulfill their sexual desires. But they are better off recognizing that they have them.

Many older women in this country are bitterly discontented. They constitute a relatively new and little-recognized class of feminists. Despite great improvements in the social and economic well-being of the elderly as a whole, older women, who outlive men an average of eight years, are still highly susceptible to poverty, depression, and isolation. I have met many older women who once lived comfortable middle-class lives, but are now living with their Social Security check their only income. Those who spent their younger years working in the home as wives and mothers find their lifelong work suddenly devalued. In many cases their husbands have died and their children have moved away.

In 1972 the National Organization for Women asked me to chair a workshop on older women at their national conference in Washington, D.C. The conference room was packed and an intense discussion ensued. Many of the women were "displaced homemakers" whose lives had been suddenly transformed by divorce, separation, or widowhood, politicizing them overnight. Seated in the back of the room was a tall, stunning woman in her sixties who periodically stood up and succinctly articulated the frustrations and goals of the group. Everyone perked up their ears when she spoke. When the workshop was over, she came forward and introduced herself as Tish Sommers.

It was the beginning of a great friendship and collaboration. Tish, the former wife of a college professor, had enormous charisma and energy. She joined the Gray Panthers and I helped her organize the Older Womens League early in 1979 with headquarters in Washington, D.C. Until her death from cancer a few years ago, she waged a determined fight to improve pension and Social Security benefits for widows and divorcées. The battle has not yet been won.

Many women who have depended on their husbands' incomes for support still find themselves relatively unprotected when their husbands die. It is no accident that while women constitute 63 percent of the elderly in this country, they are 73 percent of the elderly living below the poverty line. These statistics are a sad comment on how little women's traditional work is valued. The Social Security system does not adequately compensate women for their years working in the home. And in many cases, a man must agree to lower his pension benefits while he's alive in order to provide survival benefits for his wife after his death.

I remember the poignant case of a widow in the Minneapolis Gray Panthers who had been happily married to a successful department store executive and had led a comfortable upper-middle-class life. With her husband's death, she was shocked to learn that he had opted for higher pension benefits during his lifetime instead of leaving a pension for her. She had nothing but Social Security to carry her through her many years without him.

Why had she been so trusting? That widow's friends in the Gray Panthers said that in her old age she was finally "finding herself." For most of her life, she had relied completely on her husband, who paid all the bills and made the decisions. With his death, she was like a college student out on her own for the first time and discovering a new sense of self.

Many older women suffer deeply from the dramatic changes that occur in late life and feel a lost sense of purpose. I remember the words of Lucille Shuck, a Gray Panther member whose husband and mother died within six months of each other: "At sixty-one, no one needed me. Being needed as a daughter, wife, and mother had been my identity. I had lived vicariously. In a way, I had died with them." She survived her identity crisis and found that even at her age, one can be born again.

I believe the conditions of older women are among the most pressing problems contemporary feminism faces, and yet, too often the women's movement has focused on the needs of the younger woman trying to get ahead in the world. Younger women have lost sight of the special qualities of their grandmothers and mothers, qualities that can survive in a world of "working women."

The older women I have known and loved are

people who have endured. They have a certain perseverance and staying power that I think comes from having lovingly reared children. It takes time and enormous patience to rear a child, and the women of my generation devoted themselves to the task with all their minds and hearts. Many have also nursed their aging parents and husbands with the same selfless devotion. They have kept the world from falling apart so that working men and women like me could leave the house every day. I feel that this transcendent quality is desperately needed in the public arena.

CHAPTER 9

Shared Housing

A couple of years ago, I made a speech about my work with the Gray Panthers before a community forum at the University of Illinois at Springfield. As I was packing my papers to leave the podium, a small child approached me. She smiled and then said she had a question, a "personal" question, that she didn't dare ask in front of the entire audience. I braced myself.

"I'd like to know what your favorite TV show was when you were my age," she said.

I asked her age and she replied proudly, "I am six."

"Well," I said, "I'm afraid we didn't have television when I was your age." She looked very disappointed. "Did you have radio?" she asked.

"No, not radio," I replied. "We didn't even have a telephone at the house until I was eight." She gasped. "How awful! What did you do?" I told her we read a lot and wrote letters. She was clearly appalled. "You must read books, too," I said, seeking some common ground. "No," she said emphatically, "I watch TV." With that, we exchanged smiles again and she walked away, shaking her head.

At times it seems as if those of us who were born

at the beginning of the century and those who were born in the past twenty or thirty years have little in common. We wore high-button shoes, cranked our cars, traveled on steam engines, drank lemonade, and played whist. That little girl is growing up with Nikes, front-wheel drive, jets, Coke, MTV, and computers. We are, in many ways, from different planets.

But I believe our worlds are different only in particulars. Her future and my past include many of the same basic struggles. If she is to have a good life, she'll have to stake out her happiness much in the same way I have mine. It is more crucial today than ever that the generations know and understand each other. When the young and old feel their differences are so immense that they can't communicate, the dialogue between the past and future—a dialogue that is essential to a humane and civilized world—is cut off.

When I think of all the children who have little meaningful contact with old people, I fear for the world. Perhaps there is a correlation between the anxieties and emotional disturbances in very young children and teenagers and the lack of relationships with old people in their lives. Many of today's children are living in stress-filled homes, with parents who are competitive and striving, caught up in a web of exaggerated, unrealizable hopes. Grandma and Grandpa have time, and, often, a deeper perspective. When they are not around, that perspective is lost. As Simone de Beauvoir wrote in *The Coming of Age*,

> The whole meaning of our life is in question in the future that is waiting for us. If we do not

know what we are going to be we cannot know what we are; let us recognize ourselves in this old man or that old woman. It must be done if we are to take upon ourselves the entirety of our human state.

Indeed, people feel the distance between the generations in their daily lives. The close extended family is a rarity today. Our way of life segregates the old and young into entirely separate communities. A thirty-one-year-old woman wrote to me in 1973:

> I was raised very close to and was greatly influenced by my grandparents. We have recently moved from Seattle (where our children's grandparents are) to Ohio. I strongly feel the need and importance of the extended family for us and these older persons. What can I do? There is a retirement home very near and I wonder if we could share and learn with these folks. I very much feel we need them as much as they need us.

In my own life, I have found it possible to bridge the small differences between myself and people much younger. When I bought my house in 1958, I invited two University of Pennsylvania students to live with me. It was the wisest decision I could have made. In exchange for low rent, they took care of Sam while I was away. I discovered that I enjoyed sharing my home with young people. I appreciated my new companions, not just for their assistance, but for their company, their keen observations, their sense of humor and their excitement for life. And I have always loved a full house, with its background sounds of banging doors, feet running up and down the staircase, pans clanking in the kitchen. I like the sort of commotion that prevailed many years ago in my grandmother's house in Buffalo.

It occurred to me that this was an ideal way to live out my old age. So many of this country's elderly find themselves lost in big empty houses and resign themselves to isolation. I did not want to be in the same depressing situation. I have always been, in many ways, a family person and, once I had no close relatives alive, I decided I would start a family of my own—a family of choice.

While Elma left in 1975, Linda continued to live with me. In 1976 a young couple, Bob Jaffee and Bobbie Granger, both activists and graduate students whom I got to know through the Philadelphia Gray Panthers, moved into the third floor above my bedroom. I loved them dearly. On Saturday nights we would all stay up late watching *Saturday Night Live*, laughing, and eating popcorn. Bob, who was studying political science at the University of Pennsylvania, enjoyed ardent discussions about political theory that reminded me of my days in the Young Socialist League in Cleveland.

One Thanksgiving we added all the leaves to my dining room table and invited Bob's parents to dinner. We served turkey and tofu. Everyone managed to have a good time while skirting the issue that Bob and

Bobbie were not married. In time we had a wedding in the house, with Bob and Bobbie standing in front of the stained glass window on the first floor of my house next door. Over the course of their nine-and-a-half-year stay, they would also change their respective careers and have a baby daughter, Nicole. They finally left to go to a house of their own. We will always be friends.

I eventually bought the twin house adjoining mine with the idea of using it for office space and converting it into small apartments. Linda Horn moved over to the twin house when the renovation was done. In 1980 Anne Eagan, a young woman who was studying to become a minister at Princeton Theological Seminary, came to live on the second floor of my side of the house, while Bob and Bobbie still lived on the third floor. Anne and I were friends from the day we met. She had been a Red Cross worker in Korea. With my background in the Presbyterian Church, she often looked to me for perspective on her own experience.

Every once in a while, Anne and I would go on a clothes shopping spree. We both wore the same size so we coordinated our outfits with the idea of trading. We would go to some fancy stores: Talbots in Chestnut Hill, Lord & Taylor, and Bonwit Teller. Anne, who also helped me select an Oriental rug for the living room, liked to say that I was a socialist with a taste for the good things in life.

It was Anne who sat me down one day and suggested that I stop driving for safety's sake. I had been a good driver of fifty years with no accidents until I sideswiped a car one evening when driving home from a downtown meeting. I loved to drive, and giving up my driver's license was a wrenching rite of passage! Anne knew how much driving meant to me and I knew that she was right. We both cried that day. I still carry my expired driver's license in my wallet, but it is now an artifact.

I am not a parent figure to my young housemates. I don't keep track of their comings and goings or advise them on how to lead their lives. I like to talk to them about my life and listen to them talk about theirs. I think many adults—middle-aged or older—unthinkingly patronize the young, placing little value on their opinions and wrongly believing that experience is the root of all wisdom. That's not to say that those of us who have lived a long time can't offer some perspective to the young. By talking to people in their sixties, seventies, and eighties, young people can get a sense that bad times come and go, that history and large social forces play a part in their personal dramas, and that life is finite.

I like what Otto Luening, the composer and former professor at Columbia University, said in an interview with the Gray Panther newspaper *The Network*. Leuning noted that many of his professional relationships dissolved when he retired from the university, while friendships with his young graduate students blossomed. "I found . . . that I had a rather natural relationship with most people under thirty," he said. "They had not yet been carried away into the active workforce. While they were building their lives and trying to enter into the career stream, I was building a new life as a retired person."

Indeed people at either end of the age spectrum have a lot in common. Both young and old have trouble getting jobs and keeping them. The young because it is assumed they have no experience, and the old because their experience is deemed "useless." Both the old and the young are caught in conflict with the middle generation—the young with their parents, the old with their children. Both are going through bodily changes—losing hair or growing hair. And they both have a hard time getting credit and insurance.

Anne, Bob, and Bobbie were among a long series of housemates I've had over the years. I've always been impressed by the infinite variety of humankind, the endless permutations, and I'm very grateful that I can accept diversity and revel in it. There is no such thing as a carbon copy—and wouldn't it be dull if there were. At times the human scene has been its most picturesque within the walls of my own home. I recall the Franciscan priest who arrived at my house with a carload of books and his Norwegian elkhound, Solvaag. Sent by a mutual friend of ours, he came for a week and stayed six months, working on a doctoral study of the Book of Deuteronomy.

On weekends he was joined by a nun who, from what we could tell, slept with him on the pull-out couch in the living room. Solvaag and our cat, Toby, had territorial conflicts that were only resolved when the priest departed for a parish in the Southwest. Last year I received a note from him inviting me to a party celebrating his twenty-fifth year in the priesthood.

In time my experiment in group living became a political statement. I founded a new national organization, the National Shared Housing Resource Center, to promote the idea of "shared housing." I passionately believe that there must be more of these sorts of living arrangements. The old have been brainwashed to believe that it is safer and nicer to be with their peers in retirement communities or age-segregated organizations. Indeed, for some that may be the answer, but for increasing numbers, I believe it is not. Many old people find such arrangements confining and bleak. They want to be around young people. And young people want to be with them.

For the old there must be some alternative to living with relatives, living alone, and institutionalization. For the young, especially college students and men and women in their twenties, there needs to be a wider range of affordable places to live, places that feel like home and offer contact with older adults.

In 1980 I invited Dennis Day Lower, a young Presbyterian minister, to come to Philadelphia and work as the first director of the National Shared Housing Resource Center. At the time there was a growing number of small organizations around the country, many of them started by Gray Panthers, that were promoting the same kind of living arrangements I had. These groups ran matching services, finding suitable young people to live with older people in their houses. Dennis and I wanted the Resource Center to coordinate these programs and lobby on their behalf, as well as to work as a matching service in Philadelphia. Many of the matching programs have had to work against zoning ordinances that prohibit unrelated people from living together. These ordinances are designed to keep boarding homes out of residential neighborhoods.

Dennis, who had set up a shared house in Boston's Back Bay, arrived on my doorstep one day in January with his wife, Donna, their sheepdog, Gandoff, and a U-Haul truck holding all their worldly possessions. Starting out with a four-thousand-dollar grant from the Presbyterian Church, Dennis built a national organization.

The program now fills the basement and first and second floors of my adjoining twin house. It works with five hundred programs nationwide and has brought thousands of people together in shared houses. I feel great comfort when I think of all the people I know who have been brought together by shared-housing programs: the old man in Kansas City who took a nursing student as his housemate and gained a "niece"; the pregnant college student in New Hampshire who went to live with a widow who had never had children of her own; the California music teacher who shared her house and piano with music students.

The Shared Housing Resource Center has saved some big old houses and run-down neighborhoods along the way. A few years ago the former rectory for St. Peter's Episcopal Church in Germantown, a beautiful structure designed by the famous Philadelphia architect Frank Furness, with a giant wraparound porch, fifteen rooms, and five fireplaces, was vacant and dilapidated. In the best sort of public-private partnership, the Resource Center joined with a local developer and the Episcopal Church to renovate the property and establish a shared house. Today eight people live there; the youngest is twenty-two and the oldest is seventy-three. There is an important distinction between a house like this and a boarding house. At St. Peter's people share meals, chores, and free time. There is a real sense of togetherness and homeyness.

This sort of living arrangement isn't for everyone. Some people don't like the idea of sharing a home with strangers, fearing, among other things, a loss of privacy. They say only walruses can live on top of each other; not people, we need space. My houses are set up so that the private quarters are separate from the common areas, affording opportunities for both socializing and solitude. It has always been clear that we each have our own life to lead. We don't hold house meetings or adhere to strict meal schedules. People come and go as they please. Sometimes our only communication during the course of the day is a note written on the yellow pad on the kitchen counter.

There have been disappointments, failures, and conflict in my shared housing experience, as there are in all human relationships and endeavors. At one point two men moved into one of the small apartments next door. They were lovers and one of them had a volatile personality. Though he had been arrested and convicted in the stabbing of his former lover, we tried to sympathize with him and under-stand his troubles. When he went to prison to serve his sentence, we visited him. When he returned, he and his friend had violent arguments that held the rest of the house in terror. I finally had to ask them to leave. It was the only time I have ever asked anyone to move out.

I would like to see at least a ten year moratorium on all senior high-rises and age-segregated retirement homes built by churches, synagogues, and other pri-vate groups, with that money put into developing new kinds of living arrangements. Shared housing will never be a complete solution to the housing problems of either the old or young. It is one good alternative. When it comes to housing, I think people too often think in terms of larger and newer buildings. When I went to Greece years ago for an international confer-ence sponsored by the American Institute of Planners, we met with the famous Greek planner Constantine A. Doxiadis, who was harshly critical of American architecture and urban planning. "Everything violates human scale," he said. "You Americans think too big."

During the '70s and '80s, the Gray Panthers started dozens of other programs that, like shared housing, brought young and old together. In Madison, Wiscon-sin, for instance, they started a program for latchkey children, who, when they arrive home from school telephone an older volunteer to talk about their day.

Today *intergenerationalism* is almost a household word. Schools, nursing homes, day care centers, senior centers, Girl Scouts, and civic organizations are all exploring ways to bring the generations together. Some of the resulting programs have built true and lasting friendships, the sort of bonds that once took place within the extended family. In Philadelphia the center for Intergenerational Living, run by my friend, Professor Nancy Henkin of Temple University, matches first-time juvenile offenders in Philadelphia with older mentors who are reformed criminals. The organization also brings retired tradesmen into vocational schools to teach. The possibilities are limitless.

By 1981 the Gray Panthers occupied an entire three-story building on Chestnut Street in west Philadelphia near the University of Pennsylvania. We had a paid full-time executive staff of six, a budget of about $500,000, ninety chapters across the country, and a dues-paying membership of 9,000. We mailed our bimonthly newspaper to 60,000 subscribers.

The Gray Panthers no longer had to fight to have many of the interests of the old recognized. There had been an amazing increase in the awareness of the problems of old age and organizations working on behalf of the old represented a major political force. However, beginning in the late '70s, as the federal deficit grew, there was a backlash against progressive programs to aid the old. Politicians made headlines charging that the elderly were consuming an undeserved share of the federal budget. A new stereotype of the aged emerged. Instead of poor, dependent, helpless, and senile, the old are often seen today as rich, independent, healthy, and carefree. The typical retiree is believed to be in Florida cultivating a tan or hitting golf balls. Greedy geezers.

There are indeed retirees who fit this stereotype, people who care for nothing but their own personal satisfaction and leisure time. I remember once meeting the mayor of St. Petersburg, Florida, who complained that he could get none of the town's older residents to run for election, or advise him as a "Council of Elders." The people he approached were too busy traveling—going north in the summer, taking cruises in the winter. The mayor concluded that he had a constituency of "irresponsible gypsies."

However, the notion that the old are, by and large, an affluent group is wrong. Even with Social Security benefits, in 1989 40.5 percent of all those over sixty-five lived at 200 percent or less of the official poverty line for the aged, according to recent Social Security Administration figures. That means an income of less than $12,000 a year. More than 11 percent live below the poverty line.

Nevertheless, in the '80s, some conservatives began to argue that federal programs for the old were depriving future generations. I like to call this thinking "lifeboat logic." It was as if the American population was adrift in a lifeboat and somebody had to be dumped overboard to save the rest. This notion was given credence by academia when Samuel Preston, a sociologist at the University of Pennsylvania, made his

debut on the subject in an article that appeared in
Scientific American in December 1984. After compar-
ing the old and the young on every conceivable basis
from standard of living to suicide attempts, he concluded that "the well-being of the elderly has greatly
improved whereas that of the young has deteriorated." He maintained that many federal expenditures for the old were unwise. "Whereas expenditure
on the elderly can be thought of mainly as consumption, expenditure on the young is a combination of
consumption and investment," he wrote.

Some conservative analysts contended that Social
Security would be so bankrupt in forty years there
would be nothing left for future generations. Americans for Generational Equity, an organization formed
in 1985 by Senator David Durenberger and Representative James R. Jones to represent the supposedly
threatened interests of baby boomers, contended that
"the immense baby-boom generation—the 78 million
born between 1946 and 1964—will collectively face a
disastrous retirement, and its children will, in turn, be
much more heavily burdened with the support of its
parents than any other generation in our nation's history."

The debate over Social Security in the early '80s,
which continues to a lesser degree today, exaggerated
tensions between the generations. Social Security is a
widely misunderstood income protection program for
the old, the disabled, and for families who face sudden
illness or death. Unlike welfare, Social Security's
monthly stipends are based on the amount of Social

Security taxes the head of a household has had deducted from past paychecks. All Americans who have worked are entitled to benefits once they have reached age sixty-five and the bulk of benefits go to the old. I believe Social Security is one of the most remarkable and well-managed social programs this country has ever seen. Yet it has always been an affront to those who believe the marketplace can serve people's needs best. When Ronald Reagan came into office in 1980, his administration began to set its sights on reducing Social Security benefits, falsely linking these with the growing federal deficit (in fact, because Social Security is a self-supporting system, the two have nothing to do with each other).

Social Security benefits are hardly excessive. In 1981 about 30 percent of all elderly people living alone had annual incomes below $4,099. Monthly benefits for retired workers at the beginning of 1981 averaged $342, for elderly widows they averaged $311, and for disabled workers, $371.

Provoking an outcry by thousands of individuals and national organizations like the Gray Panthers and the AARP, Reagan's proposed Social Security cuts were never approved by Congress. However, I think the debate over Social Security during that period weakened public confidence in the program and promoted the erroneous notion that the old were depleting the nation's resources.

Though Social Security benefits have increased since the early '80s, the situation remains much the same today. Monthly benefits for retired workers av-

erage $603; for elderly widows they average $557; and
for disabled workers, $587. Only about 12 percent of
recipients fall into the category of having individual
annual incomes of $25,000 or more ($30,000 or more
for a couple), and their benefits are taxed.

I believe the intergenerational war over federal
benefits, which continues to this day, is a charade to
divert attention from the real budgetary issues. We do
not need to take from the young to feed the old or take
from the old to feed the young. There will be enough
for everyone if the federal government ends its love
affair with military hardware and extravagant tax
breaks to the rich.

Horace Deets, executive director of the American
Association of Retired Persons, said it well:

> One reason for America's greatness is that
> through our history one generation has helped
> another. Sometimes it has been through direct
> family support. Other times, indirectly
> through programs like Social Security and
> Medicare, Guaranteed Student Loans or Head
> Start. With the many problems our nation
> faces, Americans of all ages must work to-
> gether as never before. Those who try to divide
> us along age lines are doing us a great disser-
> vice.

I can't understand or sympathize with people who
think of government only in terms of what it does for
them personally. That includes both the old who vote

down school budget increases because they don't have any children in school and the young who gripe about Social Security because it doesn't do anything for them now.

The elderly lobby has been forceful and effective in preserving benefits for the old. I would like to see it speak out as powerfully on behalf of the nearly 14 million children who now constitute 40 percent of the nation's poor. One of every five American children lives in poverty. Our most promising resource for the future, our children, is now our poorest. We have never made a long-term commitment to children comparable to Social Security's commitment to the old. Instead, the young have been at the mercy of the political priorities of those in power. I feel strongly that the old must not simply advocate on their own behalf. We must act as the elders of the tribe, looking out for the best interests of the future and preserving the precious compact between the generations.

CHAPTER 10

Reflections

Take four cans of cat food. Divide them between two plastic shopping bags. Now tie the plastic bags onto both ends of a cane. Put your arms straight out. Lift the cane up as high as you can go. Up and down. Up and down. Isn't that invigorating? Now put your hands on your shoulders and flap your arms. Flap them ten times. Good. Now take four deep breaths. Ahh. Air, even the air indoors, is so sweet.

Congratulations, you have just completed the Maggie Kuhn Workout. It's the perfect way to start the day—if you are eighty-five years old. Leave time for a bubble bath afterward! Try it very warm with bubbles stacked about halfway to the ceiling. I *believe* in bubble baths. Everyone, no matter how busy or important, should start the day in a tub of bubbles. It soothes the mind and the soul. Does George Bush take bubble baths? Does Gorbachev? Probably not. The world would be better off if they did. Only when I'm sitting in the bath do I feel disconnected from my body, with its constant fits and starts.

It seems only yesterday that I could dash up and down the stairs. Up and down. Up and down. I could rush out the front door, put my key in the ignition and go. I could twist open jars, push through heavy doors, climb into the bathtub myself and see the pictures hanging on the wall in the next room. These are little things we take for granted when we are young and strong.

Today, I approach each day determined but uncertain. Will a dizzy spell catch me on the stairs? Will I be able to negotiate high curbs and get into a waiting car? How bad will the accumulated aches and pains be? Life at eighty-five years is very different. Different, of course, from twenty-five and thirty-five, but also different from sixty-five and seventy-five. The losses accumulate: the bones weaken, the eyes grow dim, the ears disappoint. "Maggie," a friend of mine says, "you are more spirit than body."

Yet, I like to think that I still have the upper hand. And so, on the helping arm of a friend, I am out the door to attend meetings in New York, Massachusetts, California, Ohio—wherever I am of use. You won't find me confined to a chair.

There are bound to be little detours and adventures along the way. I have always been fairly small, but now I am tiny, just eighty-five pounds. One day not long ago, I stepped out of a building at the United Nations and a gust of wind came and lifted me off my feet. If I hadn't been holding on to a friend's arm, I would have been blown down First Avenue.

I am what gerontologists call "old old," a member of the fastest-growing age group in America. Census figures show that more and more people are living to eighty-five and ninety in reasonably good health. We have entered what the French call "l'age troisieme." For us, the independence we make a fetish of in our society is no longer possible. We must replace independence with interdependence. Very few of us can get through the day without some assistance. We may need help cutting our food, taking a bath, getting into bed, using the toilet. No longer able to get along with two legs, I need a third—my sturdy cane.

When I think of all those ancient bones that archaeologists and paleontologists dig up—dinosaur bones and Neanderthal skulls—I am amazed at their survival. My bones, weakened by osteoporosis, crumble like saltines. Two years ago my eleventh vertebrae collapsed, eliminating my waistline and depositing my ribcage on my pelvis. I have a pronounced hump on my back—a classic example of what they call a "dowager's hump"—and my arthritic fingers are so infirm I have difficulty cutting meat or buttering bread.

Life is complicated by what my doctors call "macrodegeneration," or deterioration of the retinas. Sitting on the couch in my living room, I have difficulty seeing clearly what's in the kitchen. I know that the pans are hanging up there and that there is the microwave, but I can't see them in detail. Outside I am very sensitive to light. I always carry my sunglasses and wear them on what some people might call an overcast day. I used to love being in the sun, particularly to walk in the sun, but now the light blinds me.

What *can* we do, those of us who have survived to this advanced age? We can think and speak. We can remember. We can give advice and make judgments.

We can dial the phone, write letters, and read. We may not be able to butter our bread, but we can still change the world.

We can think and we can speak. Indeed, we can speak! "Must you do this?" my assistant, Sue, sometimes asks, pointing to my crowded calendar. I can hear my bones ask the same question. "Absolutely!" I respond. "I absolutely must." For though I am—by anybody's reckoning—near the end of my life, I still have a certain drive to get out there, to have my opinion heard, to get things done. There is still so very much to get done.

Those of us who are old can also still love. Just a short time ago, my dear friend Marilyn moved to Israel, and for a while, I felt a great sense of loss. Perhaps my love of my friends is stronger at this stage of life. I must confront the nagging question—how much longer do we have together? Sometimes I even still feel that old familiar tug. A male friend of mine often squeezes my hand and asks, "So when are we going to have a love affair?" It's a tempting offer.

"Age does not mean moving out," says my friend and fellow Gray Panther Mildred Sklar. "One takes part by giving one's presence, by writing the encouraging note, by calling a meeting to discuss and clarify an issue, by saying the healing, binding, or forward-looking phrase in a conversation, by phoning when there is a hiatus in communication. We have the possibility of altering the character of life by our own actions, however small they may seem."

For me, this is a glorious period of life. More than

anything else, old age has fed my passions—my passion for the world, for people, for a better way. As my personal tale is about to end, I am more interested than ever in the larger story. I am free in a way that was not possible when I was thirty or forty.

Looking back, I think the most stressful year of my life came with my thirtieth birthday. My God, thirty seemed so old. And most people at thirty were married. I can see now more than I could then how troubled I was—not because I was single, but because everyone seemed to suddenly view me as odd. People would constantly say, "You're not married?" And they would ask my mother, "She's not married? That's strange."

And at the age of sixty-four, when I faced retirement, I was apprehensive and, in a sense, depressed because so much of my life had been invested in my work. And not to have a job, not to have a structure that you're part of, was very, very hard for me to accept. Now there is none of that stress and anxiety.

Old age is not a disaster. It is a triumph over disappointment, failure, loss, illness. When we reach this point in life, we have great experience with failure. I always know that if one of the things that I've initiated falters and fails, it won't be the end. I'll find a way to learn from it and begin again. When I was younger, I took failure much more seriously.

As Simone de Beauvoir noted almost twenty years ago, the issues of age challenge the whole of society and put it to the test. Indeed, those of us who are very old and frail are a reminder to the world of the delicate interdependence of us all. We are more human than ever before because we see so clearly how finite life is. Unfortunately, those of us who are dependent, handicapped, or old are often deemed a separate species. If you happen to be an old person accompanied by a middle-aged person in a restaurant and you show even just a hint of deafness or uncertainty in your step, you are not going to be addressed by the head waiter. You are going to be talked right past like a child—"What does she want to eat today?" The same thing happens to people in wheelchairs.

All of us are at the mercy of circumstance and fate. But when we have reached our ninth decade and when the biggest transition of all—death—lies just before us, we are better at surrendering to life. It is not resignation but acceptance. We have learned that change is a constant.

My gardener, Leon Majors, has deepened my appreciation of change. Over the years Mr. Majors has transformed the scraggly plot of grass in the back of my house. There are azaleas in the spring, tiger lilies in the summer, chrysanthemums in the fall, and varieties of frost, ice, rain, and snow on the trees and bushes in winter. Mr. Majors has lived most of his life in the poor inner city. Being a gardener in the heart of the city takes vision. Indeed, Mr. Majors is more than a gardener; he's a philosopher and preacher. One of his themes is that the seed is a very special part of life, a symbol. If you look at the tiny seed, you can see so little of all the changes to come. "A seed possesses in itself a mature tree in a miniature state," Mr. Majors tells me. "We just can't see it. If the conditions are right, it's just a matter of time once the tree is planted before it unfolds itself and reveals its history. There are small seeds that produce large trees and large seeds that produce small trees."

When I look at my garden, it is not so much the individual parts I appreciate as the changing whole. And so it is with my life. I have not yet revealed all of my history.

Two years ago, on a Tuesday evening in November, I came in close contact with the cold, hard streets of Philadelphia. I remember it vividly. Diane Carlson, one of my housemates at the time, came into the house on her way to a play rehearsal as I was preparing to go out. I said, "Well, I'm on my way to the neighborhood meeting." She said, "I'll walk you down there."

The meeting of our neighborhood civic association was to be held at Stapley Hall, a retirement home just a block from my house. It was raining in torrents. Diane had the umbrella over us and I was hanging on to her right arm and she had a big purse over her left shoulder. We were just turning into the driveway of Stapley Hall when all of a sudden I was knocked to the ground. It was a sharp blow, as if I had been hit by a car. I found myself lying facedown. I called, "Diane, Diane, where are you?" I couldn't see her or feel her. There was a moment of shock. "Here I am," she called out, and I felt her hand on my head. "Damn," she said. "Some kids just ran off with my purse. We've been mugged."

I couldn't move. I had a hat on and a thin coat and felt very cold there on the rainy sidewalk. Diane ran into Stapley Hall and told them what had happened. Arriving with a wheelchair and umbrella, my neighbors picked me up and wheeled me to shelter. My shoulder was in great pain. I hurt everywhere and was trembling violently.

I spent a week in the hospital recovering from bruises and a broken shoulder. My face looked as if I had been in a boxing match. They put my arm in a sling and the pain was excruciating. Because of my age—I was eighty-three years old—the recovery time was prolonged.

Of course, they never found the two young boys. I never expected them to nor did I feel a great desire to see them apprehended. Many people asked me if I felt angry and outraged at the boys who mugged us. "No," I said emphatically. "I pity those boys. What an awful life they must lead." It is cliché to say so, but I believe those boys are the real victims. The root causes of the problem are visible all around us: the failing schools, the lack of federal monies for city programs, the unemployment rate.

I have lived in Philadelphia now for almost sixty years and have great affection for my city. I've seen my neighborhood fall from prosperity to grim subsistence and then waver between revival and decay, yet have never lost faith in my neighborhood's capacity for improvement. As I reach the end of my life, I feel an urgent need to give something back to my home city, to repay it for the good things it has done for me. If I could give it anything, I'd give it hope.

The prevailing view in so many American cities today is one of hopelessness. Many of the problems of urban life—the crime, the poverty, the illiteracy—seem overwhelming. And one devastating consequence of the very bigness of our cities, our institutions, and our social organizations is that individuals feel more powerless to bring about change. Yet, as a college biology student, I was always impressed by the antibodies—the little things that have the capacity to heal. In general, I am not impressed by grand solutions. If people start on their own front step, they come to realize that big problems can be tackled with lots of solutions.

I think it is easier to have hope when one is very old. One sees that over the course of time, people have managed to overcome countless difficulties with amazing resourcefulness. Not long ago, a few friends and I started the Commission on the Future of Philadelphia. "The future of Philadelphia?" people ask. We want to prod the public to think about what lies ahead, to dream instead of reacting to crises as they occur. As part of our work, Evo Giomi, a retired schoolteacher who is my neighbor, arranged to have children in a number of schools create their own artistic representations of the city for an exhibit. It was a brilliant idea.

I remember one entry in particular. A group of fifth graders made a huge clay model of the city. It was four times the size of my coffee table and was beautifully painted, with little boats on the Delaware River and City Hall and Liberty Place and even a homeless shelter and a crack house. It was the city in all its vitality. It occurred to me as I looked at the model that part of the duty of a civic activist is to bring out the beauty of a place, to show that even a city that needs great improvement has great virtues.

Last summer, during a hot spell, officials at Ben & Jerry's Ice Cream called from their office in Vermont to inform me I was the latest recipient of their "Pints of Light" Award, given to a citizen who has demonstrated civic pride. I had won one thousand pints of "light" ice cream. Fortunately, I am an avid ice cream consumer. "We'll be down next week with the ice cream," they said. "Fine," I said.

I was happy to accommodate the award ceremony in front of my house. Jerry came with two young assistants in a truck that was painted to look like a pasture with two cows grazing in the grass. It could barely fit down our narrow cobblestoned street.

A little yellow tent was set up and coolers of ice cream were brought out to the sidewalk. It was a rainy day, but people from all over the neighborhood were drawn to the goings-on in front of my house. I gave ice cream to everyone who passed and soon there was a jolly crowd on my city street. Everyone was laughing and talking and eating ice cream. I was thrilled. I wish I could be out there more often, handing out ice cream to passers-by.

On May 10, 1990, I boarded an Amtrak train for Washington, D.C., and headed to the twentieth annual convention of the Gray Panthers. On the train with me were a number of my colleagues. There was Jean Hopper, our librarian, and ninety-year-old Doris Campbell, a member of our Camden, New Jersey, chapter who came to the station alone with her luggage and her walker. Several members of our New York group met us on the train.

When we got to Union Station in Washington, there was great discussion and debate. Wherever there are Gray Panthers, there is great discussion and debate. Some of us wanted to head right for the 4-H Center in Chevy Chase, where the convention was to be held. Others wanted to head for a demonstration on Capitol Hill. Still others wanted lunch. Eventually, we broke off into subgroups to attend to our different needs. Wherever there are Gray Panthers, there are task forces.

The convention was a four-day affair, with speakers, business sessions and workshops every day from 8:00 A.M. to midnight. Gray Panther conventions are generally all business. We are an organization that never quite feels we have done enough. There were meetings on our major concerns, such as health care, housing, intergenerational programs, pension rights, and the decline of responsible philanthropy, as well as on a number of other less pressing issues. There were representatives from the organizations we had helped to found: the Older Women's League, the Black Caucus for the Aged, the National Shared Housing Resource Center, and the National Coalition for Nursing Home Reform. All in all, two hundred people attended—a good turnout these days—and Ralph Nader delivered an inspiring opening address.

The crowd was noticeably older than in years past. The organization has aged with me, and many of our members are in their late seventies and eighties. You would not mistake a Gray Panther convention for, let's say, a gathering of retired business executives discussing their investment portfolios. The men and women at the 4-H Center had natural gray hair and sported running shoes, faded denim skirts, berets, and Greek sailor caps. They were a contentious bunch, prone to shout out and interrupt each other during committee meetings. They are used to making their opinions known. Though there was constant debate and disagreement, the convention was a happy, uplifting affair—like a family reunion. A sense of camaraderie and shared values prevailed.

"Retirement is like being rich," one of my fellow Gray Panthers has said. "Nobody can fire you." Indeed, many of our members consider the organization's work the most fulfilling job of their lives, a true labor of love.

I am still the organization's "convener," or inspirational leader and spokeswoman. Over the years our group has seen its membership and budget decline. We have closed our office in Philadelphia, moving our headquarters to Washington, D.C., in the hope of gaining a greater voice in national affairs. I believe our smaller membership is, in part, a sign that we have done our job well. We have gotten much of our original message across and succeeded in bringing about major changes in the way the old are perceived and treated.

In other ways we have not succeeded. Not yet. We

have not succeeded in demonstrating to the public that we are concerned about a variety of larger societal issues, as well as the problems of the old. In a country divided by special interest groups and single-issue strategies, it has been difficult to convey that we are a group with many goals. We are, for instance, one of the few large organizations pressing for a publicly supported national health system that would provide comprehensive, free, and accessible health care for all. We are working to make the American workplace more flexible to accommodate the schedules of people of all ages so that employees can take sabbaticals in mid-life or stay on the job in late life. We are also trying to gain public understanding of the ongoing work of the U.N., where we have nongovernmental observation status, to "harmonize the differences" between nation states.

I've sometimes infuriated my co-workers at the Gray Panthers by taking on new causes. Over the years I've walked the picket line with children who deliver newspapers (for outrageously low pay) in Providence, Rhode Island; attended community meetings among the Indians of New Mexico; and fought to prevent General Motors from razing a working-class neighborhood in Detroit to make way for an auto plant. I've never been able to turn down a good cause. When I worked for the YWCA and the Presbyterian Church, I came to see all injustices, no matter how small or seemingly unrelated, as linked. Some Gray Panthers, especially the staff members, understandably preferred to stick to a few important issues.

Organizations that swim against the stream tend to attract some bizarre characters. Over the years we have had our share; to a certain extent, they have drained our energies and efforts. There is a judicious balance between their freedom to speak out and be a part of social change and our need as a group to get something done.

We have never had a lot of money or a lot of power. But we have learned how much you can do with modest resources and we've always enjoyed favorable press. From the start I hoped that our group would serve as a model for grass-roots activism because we managed to give our networks across the country a large degree of autonomy while preserving a national agenda.

Many people have asked me what will happen to the organization after I am gone and who will take my place. I have maintained that it's not possible for me to groom a successor. I believe someone will rise from the ranks and keep the group going in its own spirited way. Leadership emerges in response to needs and inspiration.

In my office there's a picture, given to me by the Gray Panthers staff, of a flock of sandhill cranes. These have been among my favorite birds ever since I happened to be in Hastings, Nebraska, one year in the fall, when the cranes descend on the Mississippi Delta to feed. There is something in the Delta mud that they enjoy. They come down in the spring to mate and in the fall to gather strength for the journey to the subtropics. In watching thousands of birds going about the business of migration, a great deal can be learned about human groups.

Each bird, as he feeds or courts, appears to be acting alone. Then suddenly there is some dramatic coordinated effort—and you realize that nothing has been done alone, that every action of the individual has been preparing for that great sweep of birds across the sky.

Leadership involves turbulence. The lead birds create the turbulence that enables the flock to fly. Leadership on the long journey south is shared. One crane may lead for a time, but then he falls back and his place is taken by another. The lead birds are affirmed by the honkers. "HONK, HONK, HONK!" The sound of their voices descends to the ground from far up into the sky. I think I know what they are saying: "Go, go, go! We're with you. Fly!"

Fifteen years ago, on my seventieth birthday, some young friends across the street gave me two kittens. I'll never forget my first look at those two tiny black-and-white newborns. They looked up at me with wide, imploring eyes from their little basket and I was instantly smitten.

They were mischievous cats who particularly enjoyed getting into my office on the first floor and rooting through my papers and books. We decided they had literary inclinations and named them after the Brontë sisters, Emily and Charlotte. Whenever I return home from a trip, the cats greet me in the front hall. Though others might take care of them while I'm away, I like to think they maintain a special allegiance to me. One always sleeps at the foot of my bed, the other at the head. Sometimes they alternate positions at night, like sentries on duty.

Emily and Charlotte have aged with me and it seems they visit the veterinarian now more often than I go to the doctor. They are among my dearest friends and are part of the reason why I want to remain in my own house as long as I live. When I look around my living room, it is hard to imagine it without me. There are the Oriental rugs my father bought in 1931 on the floor, my grandmother's Haviland china in the kitchen cabinet, and a lover's postcards from around the world on my bedroom wall.

Not long ago, a woman approached me during the coffee hour at church and introduced herself as the resident of a Presbyterian retirement home in suburban Philadelphia. "You don't like retirement homes, do you?" she said accusingly.

"I'm sure they are fine for some people," I replied. "But what is good for some is not always good for all." The woman walked away in a huff.

It takes some courage and determination to remain in your home when you become very old and frail. Some of my friends tell me, "You've got to get out of the house! Just look at those steps." It's true the steep curving staircase is now a hazard, but it would never cause me to leave. I have three young housemates who help me up and down the stairs—and I have Bertha.

Bertha Monroe is one of the kindest and gentlest

people I know. Every weekday morning she arrives at my house at 8:00 A.M., wearing a crisp white uniform and a warm smile. Knowing she is among their most ardent admirers, Charlotte and Emily always greet her when she steps in the door.

Bertha is a nurse's aide who travels from home to home, tending to the old. She is fifty-nine years old, a native of South Carolina and a deeply religious woman. In the mornings I'm like a car with a cold engine. I need someone there with a foot on the accelerator. Bertha helps me bathe and dress and get down the steps to the living room or out the front door.

Bertha has an inborn talent for her work, an unusual sympathy and respect for the old and their frailties. She is never grouchy or impatient, never patronizing. She knows how to lift a person into the bathtub without making her feel helpless. She imparts some of her own strength to whomever she touches.

The miraculous thing about the Berthas of the world is that they don't *have* to be so kind. There is plenty of work for nurse's aides who don't smile. And there are few tangible rewards—no prizes or riches—for those who do. This is why, I suppose, Bertha calls her work "a ministry." She has higher goals in mind.

Bertha often tells me about the other old people she sees during the course of her workday. So many are sad and lonely. It is no secret that many old people are prone to depression. The find it hard to rise above their body's failures and to find a purpose in life. I can sympathize with them. About a year ago I came the closest I have ever come to a feeling of utter helplessness.

One day I slid into the backseat of a friend's car without loosening the back of my dress. I wrenched my neck and back and, in the process, cracked my eleventh vertebra. Just like that. At my age there is drama and danger in the little things you do. I know people my age who have broken bones while changing position in bed or getting into the tub.

My back injury kept me housebound for weeks and the confinement was harder than usual because I had just recovered from a bout of pneumonia. I was in terrible pain. I would force myself to walk and then collapse into bed, exhausted from the effort. Generally, I refuse to take prescription medicine for pain. Painkillers deaden the mind along with everything else. I try to move beyond the pain by disconnecting it from my body and thinking of it as something apart from myself.

The cats comforted me. Every once in a while, Charlotte would come up and look at me, rubbing me with her whiskers, to see if I was all right. As I lay in bed, I could not keep from brooding over my future or doubting my ability to recover. This is what is hard for the old who are very sick. Each time they are confined to bed, they must wonder if they will ever be able to get up again.

The pain was unrelenting so, at the suggestion of a friend, I asked a "touch therapist" to visit me. When you're suffering, you're willing to try anything. I stretched out on the couch in my living room while she tried to heal me. She would radiate energy from her body to mine and we would think and meditate together. What a strange experience. I believe there is more healing in the human touch than all the machines and prescriptions in the world, but even the touch therapist didn't do me much good.

My physical therapist, who gave me an intensive routine of reconditioning exercises, helped the most. Even when we think our bodies can never be repaired, they prove to be amazingly resilient. The therapist taught me to do the "rock of ages." By gently rocking back and forth in a chair, gradually accelerating the pace, I learned to rise from a chair and get to a standing position without hurting my back.

Before I recovered fully, however, I had to work to keep myself from becoming depressed. I found that having a goal beyond my private concerns was the best cure. One day, as I lay in bed, I began to call friends to line up speakers for a Gray Panthers meeting. I talked to Ralph Nader, Bob Butler, Carroll Estes, and Sidney Wolfe, and I felt a little better with each call. Picking yourself up after disappointment or sickness, isn't that what life always forces us to do? Isn't there always that choice between surviving or surrendering?

In my old age I have discovered a miracle. When I reach out to others I find that I receive a new kind of energy, which is physical, mental, and spiritual. It rejuvenates and emboldens me. So many people are ashamed to ask for what they need. I have two friends who say, "Anytime you need to go anywhere, just call me." I so appreciate that. We visit with each other while we go shopping or to the doctor's. They have given me a confidence about asking for help, and now I don't hesitate to flag strangers down on the street and ask for help getting up a curb or into a car.

I am sad when I hear about very old people— women, especially, because we are the survivors— with no friends, no interests, no purpose, just a void day after day. Reaching out is so hard for many people. They are so proud. A friend told me recently about a woman in her seventies who broke her hip. After she returned home from the hospital, she never went out again. What a tragic waste. I call that woman a prisoner under house arrest. Where are her neighbors? Her friends? Her family? Her confinement is a sad commentary. There should be no prisoners of old age.

We need to turn outward—as much as we are able. Gregory Bergman, my dear friend, often talks of overcoming the terrible depression he felt upon the loss of his wife. "I totally lost my zest for life," he said. "My only desire was to join her. I felt it was too late to make a new start in life. The most helpful idea I found to combat depression came from a young woman I met. She said the pain of depression came because the 'arrow' of my attention and energy was turned inward. Unless I turned the arrow around, outward and forward in time, the pain would remain."

I was sitting on a stage facing the 1989 graduating class of the University of Pennsylvania. Beside me sat my great hero, Riccardo Muti, the renowned conductor of the Philadelphia orchestra. I have spoken to many large audiences over the years and it is second nature to me now. Muti, however, was extremely nervous that day.

He was the commencement speaker, and I was there to receive an honorary degreee. "I am scared to death," he said. "Usually it's my back facing the audience, never my front." I had seen his back many times from my seat at the Academy of Music. Those shoulders, those arms, those wonderful hands! He did not need to worry—his address was eloquent and provocative. As we rose to leave, he kissed my hand. What a thrill to receive such attention from an idol.

Music—especially Brahms, Tchaikovsky, and Beethoven—was the only thing that consistently brought a sense of peace to my brother, Sam. The four of us—my mother, father, Sam, and I—began to attend concerts at the Academy of Music forty years ago. I still have three season's tickets in the first balcony to the Tuesday evening series, which I share with friends. They are priceless to me.

Today when I go to the Academy of Music, I forget about everything else. Each part of the orchestra has its own magic—the strings, the woodwinds, the percussion. As I sit in my plush red seat and listen to the great orchestra below, our imperfect world seems beautiful. Tchaikovsky's Symphony No. 5 in E Minor is one of my favorites. After a good performance I am the first to applaud and shout "Bravo!" and the last to leave my seat. The feeling of exhilaration lingers with me for several days.

I've fantasized about where I'd like to die. Most people would like to die at home, and I guess I would like to die in my house. But if I was leaving a concert or hurrying from a meeting, a speech, or conference, that would be fine. I've done my work. Mission accomplished. I'm ready.

I don't fear death itself. I remember when my beloved cat Toby died in my lap sixteen years ago. I buried her under the azalea bush in the backyard, and it has flowered more beautifully every year since. You see, death isn't a terrible thing. I don't believe in reincarnation, but I think the spirit of each of us lingers on in this world.

Though I approach death willingly, I don't want it to come too late. As much as I am an advocate for living fully in old age, I don't believe in extending life past its natural deadline. Some people may live to be one hundred or even older and stay in reasonably good health. But I know my body would not hold up well, and so I would prefer not to live into my nineties. I have drawn up my "living will," giving the power of durable attorney to a friend. My experience with my brother taught me that no extraordinary means should be used to prolong life when it's clear it should end.

I can put up with physical limits; it's not these that I worry about. To lose one's mind and become senile—that would be the ultimate tragedy, the ultimate loss. Not to be aware of what's going on in the world and my part in it would be worse than death. I don't want to live if that happens.

We all wish to preserve some dignity to the end. Dr. Benjamin Spock, the pediatrician and a fellow advocate, put it well when he told of a small incident in his own life. "I think a lot of older people don't worry at all about death, as long as it's not too painful," he said. "But I do worry about such things as getting spots on my clothes. I once saw the architect Frank Lloyd Wright in the Plaza Hotel in New York. I went up in the elevator with him. Though he

was very dashingly dressed with a big, broad-rimmed cow-
boy hat and a flowing bow-tie, there were [food stains] all
over his clothes. That really scared me. I thought, 'I hope
I don't get to the state where I don't see them.' "

When friends come to my house to visit these days, I
often tell them to pick something among my belongings that
they would like to have when I die. I have asked them to
keep my funeral simple. You won't find me in a four-
thousand-dollar casket: a plain pine box will do. And I
would like it to be an upbeat event with lots of music. I hope
I go in the spring or summer because the service could be
held outdoors in a garden.

In the meantime I want to live a full life until my
death, to continue filling my seat at the Academy of Music,
to go on attending Gray Panthers meetings, to do something
outrageous every day. Though not original, I would like my
gravestone inscribed with the words, "Here lies Maggie
Kuhn under the only stone she left unturned." After all,
there is still so very much to be done! Whenever I feel a little
dizzy or weak, I take a sniff of some good old-fashioned
ammonia spirits. What a kick!

Bibliography

CHAPTER TWO

Cramer, C.H. *Case Western Reserve: A History of the University, 1826–1976*. Boston and Toronto: Little, Brown & Company, 1976.

Rose, William Ganson. *Cleveland: The Making of a City*. Cleveland: World Publishing Company, 1950.

CHAPTER THREE

Carner, Lucy Perkins. *The First 100 Years of the Young Women's Christian Association of Germantown, 1870-1970*. Mimeographed. Philadelphia: Young Women's Christian Association of Germantown, 1969.

Robinson, Marion O. "Eight Women of the YWCA." Mimeographed. New York: National Board of the Young Women's Christian Association of the U.S.A., 1966.

CHAPTER FOUR

Hirth, Emma P., "The History of the Participation of the YWCA in the USO, 1940–1944." Mimeographed. New York: National Board of the Young Women's Christian Association, 1948.

McCullough, Rhoda E., *Little Talks on Large Subjects*. New York: The Woman's Press, 1930.

CHAPTER FIVE

Brackenridge, Douglas. *Eugene Carson Blake: Prophet with Portfolio*. New York: Seabury Press, 1978.

Smylie, James. *American Presbyterians: A Pictorial History*. Louisville: Westminster/John Knox Press, 1985.

CHAPTER SIX

Pratt, Henry J. *The Gray Lobby*. Chicago: University of Chicago Press, 1976.

CHAPTER SEVEN

Butler, Robert N. *Why Survive? Being Old in America*. New York: Harper & Row, 1975.

de Beauvoir, Simone. *The Coming of Age*. Translated by Patrick O'Brian. New York: G.P. Putnam's Sons, 1972.

CHAPTER EIGHT

Addone, Maureen. "Post Street Post Mortum." *Gray Panther Network*, May/June 1980.

Davis, Karen, Paula Grant and Diane Rowland. "Alone and Poor—The Plight of Elderly Women." *Generations*, Summer, 1990.

Griesel, Elma and Linda Horn. *Nursing Homes: A Citizens' Action Guide*. Boston: Beacon Press, 1977.

Hall, Jane. "Old, Bold and Angry." *TV Guide*, June 21, 1975.

Hallaren, Bill. "Nobody (in TV) Loves You When You're Old and Gray," *New York Times*, July 24, 1977.